M000222756

What You Can Do...When You Can't

What You Can Do...When You Can't

Twenty-One Days To Personal Success

CAROLYN JOYCE AND DARALEE BARBERA

Contact the Authors at:
whatyoucando@icloud.com
Phone: 1.714.477.UCAN (8288)

I Can Journal:
Additional *I Can Journals* are available for purchase under separate cover.

Disclaimer:
The authors of this book do not dispense medical advice nor diagnose or prescribe treatment for physical, psychological, emotional, or medical problems. Consult a licensed professional for diagnosis and treatment, as this book is not intended to be a substitute. The intent of the authors is to provide information and suggestions of a general nature. The authors and publisher assume no responsibility or liability for the actions taken as a result of reading this book.

All rights reserved.
No part of this book may be reproduced or transmitted in any form or by any means, electronic or mechanical, including photocopying, scanning, recording, or by any information storage or retrieval system, without written permission of the authors, except for the inclusion of brief quotes in articles or reviews.

WFW Publishing, a division of Walking FilmWorks, Inc.
wfwpublishing.com

© 2015 by Carolyn Joyce and Daralee Barbera. All rights reserved.

ISBN-13: 9780985142186
ISBN-10: 0985142189
Library of Congress Control Number: 2015917809
WFW Publishing, Manhattan Beach, CA

Contents

Dedication

Carolyn

With pride and admiration, I dedicate this book to my daughters Karen and Jackie. Without their support and love, this book would not have possible. My pride pours over to my grandson Zachary who demonstrates by example an *"I Can"* attitude.

Daralee

I dedicate this book to my wonderfully supportive husband, children, and family. My extraordinary inspiration has been my parents, Darrell and Marian Larsen, who have always only seen the *"can"* in the *"can't."*

Acknowledgments

We would like to express our appreciation to our family and friends for their encouragement and support for *What You Can Do...When You Can't: Twenty-One Days to Personal Success.* Thank you to Walking FilmWorks for the many hours of help with editing and formatting. Sincere thanks to our family and friends for their invaluable input.

Preface

Life, the Greatest Journey

Life itself is the greatest journey of all. Some know their path at a young age, and some of us are still trying to figure it out. Navigating life's peaks and valleys with confidence and optimism rather than fear and foreboding helps us to enjoy every moment of the journey.

Writing this book instilled in us a feeling of joy and a reassurance that we were on target to achieve one of our long-standing goals. We are excited about writing this book because it is an opportunity to share with you some of the lessons we have learned along our life's journey and the "*I can*" choices we make every day. We decided that it was now time for us to give back by sharing with you the knowledge, experiences, and some of the choices we have applied in our lives. Writing this book has helped us realize our purpose—to share and educate.

Being better informed about yourself—who you are, where you have been, and where you want to go—can and will make a positive difference in your life. We hope you will feel like you have your own mentor and friend right beside you during this journey. Each decision you make will have an impact on everything and everyone around you, so having some guidance may help you make better choices. We hope our perspectives will make a positive difference for you as you travel down your life's path and that you will share them with your colleagues, friends, and family.

Prologue

You Can!

When you get up every morning and think about the challenges you face that day, are you excited and do you tell yourself, "*I can*"? We wrote this book because we believe you *can* face each day with confidence, optimism, and an attitude of gratitude. Our book will show you how.

Sometimes life is exhilarating, and sometimes it is stressful and daunting. Having an arsenal of strategic tools can help. We have tried what feels like an infinite number of approaches for many years in our professional and personal lives. Some worked, and some…well, not so much. In this book we share those strategies that worked for us. We have found that when we need to tackle anything, it's best to keep it as simple and easy to understand as possible. In fact, the simpler the better.

Most problems can be dealt with via a simple three-step process: *Evaluate, Formulate*, and *Act*. This approach fits into our plan to "*Keep It as Simple as 1-2-3*" on problem solving. If we let things get too complicated, we often become overwhelmed and paralyzed by the thought of failure. This accomplishes nothing. Therefore, the most complex must be translated to simpler terms. You will clearly see our approach of *Evaluate* first, *Formulate* second, and then finally *Act.*

We have lived our personal and professional lives by this approach, and we know it works. So from our hearts to yours, we invite you to share some of the exercises and ideas that we have used successfully to achieve success and peace of mind. It is our hope that one or more of them will work for you so that you can set audacious goals and accomplish them.

One

The "Job" of Living Life

Life loves to be taken by the lapel and
told, I'm with you kid. Let's go.

—Maya Angelou

On average, most people have about eleven jobs in their working lifetime, and this number is increasing. You may have had fewer or more, but there is one job that we all have in common: it's the job of living life. Life is the career we are born into, the career that matters the most out of all the other jobs we have. Although it is the most important job of one's lifetime, it is often the most neglected. We have competing priorities and a multitude of tasks demanding our attention. Some are planned, and some are not. Some are critical, and others are optional. The question we need to ask ourselves, almost moment by moment, is, "How well am I doing at this job of living life?" Your answer is critical to ensuring that you achieve the kind of accomplishments you want in your life.

Regardless of how you proceed with the job of living life, your mission is paramount. Your mission impacts everything you do and those around you. Part of the job description of living life is to live it to the best of your ability and in the best way you know how. After all, it is your life and no one else's. Being in charge of *you* is the biggest responsibility you have.

1

The fact is, you are in control, but how in charge do you actually feel? Do you feel that you are being all you can be? Would you like to do more? Would you like to do some things differently? We have found that most people have expectations for themselves that are lower than their potential. Have you ever found yourself saying, "I wish I could do that," or "I'd like to do better"?

This is a book of practical, quick, hands-on exercises—sort of an on-the-job training manual. The job, in this case, is life. Every single day we are on the job, living life. Everyday life can present us with challenges. Big or small, we must tackle them.

Often we have decisions to make, situations to deal with, and people to inter-act with, and varying skill sets are required. Sometimes it is hard to know initially what is the right thing to do. Sometimes we do not feel equipped or adequately prepared. There are strategies you can use to make it through these challenging situations.

In this rapid-fire world, where do you find the skills you don't think you have? We can all think of a time when we felt like we just couldn't figure something out, when we could actually hear ourselves saying, *"I can't."* Well, just by virtue of the fact that you are reading this book, you made it past that moment. You are on the other side. But how do you deal with moments that present themselves in a split-second fashion? This is a skill that if well-developed can lead to a better quality of life. So how do you confront life's situations when they come at you?

> *Life is like riding a bicycle; to keep your*
> *balance, you must keep moving.*
>
> —Albert Einstein

The I Can Strategy

We will share strategies that have worked for us in everyday situations and some not-so-everyday situations. For those times when it just feels like life is impossible, when you feel like you *can't* go forward, when *"I just can't"* is the first thing on your mind, just remember our practical and quick tips so that you will be saying, *"I can!"*

Some strategies work quickly, and some take more time to implement. The important thing is to move yourself from *I can't* to *I can*. It is up to you. No one can do it for you. Taking ownership of your own attitude and future is a prerequisite. Who you are, what you do, and how you act all determine how the world around you will impact your journey through life. This is where we begin.

These are practical strategies that *you can* do at those times when you really, absolutely, positively think *you can't*. Yes, we have all been there, and we probably will be again. But we want to make that journey shorter so that any negative mind-set disappears and is replaced with a positive perspective of *I can*. The key is to make smart choices and use those ideas that will help you to conquer negative self-talk.

Within these pages you will find that certain something you need to help you with your choices and provide you with the skills you need for the job of living life. Sometimes it just takes one idea to make all the difference; it can be that one thing that will help you make the changes you want to make.

Let's face it, all of the science behind what makes one strategy work and one not work is of no importance if we don't believe it is possible in our hearts. We think a belief in a positive outcome is critical to accomplishing anything.

We have found that the more we keep lessons and ideas simple and easy, the more likely we are to implement them into our daily lives. Our intention is to keep the exercises as simple as the *ABCs* or as simple as *1-2-3*. This makes it less intimating to get started, and to start is

remember
a-b-c
1-2-3

what we must do so that we can begin our journey toward *I can*. Throughout the book we will ask you questions designed to promote personal reflection. Questions are important in their own right because answers are of little value if we are not asking the right questions.

Lifelong Friends

It may sound odd to consider, but every journey you take, you take with your lifelong friends: me, myself, and I. You are always your own travel companion. Our purpose is to bring the three of you to one place, at one time, to celebrate the ultimate, one-and-only, awesome *you*. This requires being keenly in touch with who you are and how you feel about yourself. Your reaction to events and circumstances, and how you feel about them, is what we are going to work on. We want to help you understand the impact these events and circumstances have in your life.

You are in charge, and what you do with your opportunities is your responsibility. It's all up to you. This book is here to be one of your many resources. Ask yourself why you picked up this book. Whatever the reason—and there is a reason—the bottom line is that you are on a new journey, and each journey begins with one step.

Two

The Evaluation of You

The best and most beautiful things in the world cannot be seen or even touched, they must be felt with the heart.

—Helen Keller

Life is a stage, and you get only one performance. Make it a good one! First we need to understand what show we will be in and the path that our experiences will take. Surprise! The show is you! So get your act together before you put the show on the road.

What Is Your Signature? Who Are You?

The first step in any process is to *Evaluate*. The starting point involves analyzing and understanding yourself. It really all begins with you! You need to have the best possible understanding of yourself at this moment. Where are you right now? Where do you want to be? What is your destination? How are you going to get there? And finally, what do you want your outcome to be?

For example, what is your signature? Nothing is quite so personal, or individual, as your unique signature. It helps to define and express who you are.

5

As illustrative as your signature is on a page, so is your signature on life and the window that it provides.

Why fit in when you were born to stand out?

—Dr. Seuss

Why Does It Matter?

Life is not a dress rehearsal. You have one shot in this life, so why not be the best you can be?

Think about a time when you felt that you were on top of the world, and really *feel* it. How old were you? What were you doing? What do you think contributed to your success at that time?

Now imagine that you control the circumstances of your life and the stress, not the other way around. Imagine that you can surpass any challenges you are facing now and that you have that top-of-the-world feeling again. To this end, the biggest motivator is your thinking. When you believe your outcome will be positive, you are in harmony with the universe. Peace and harmony will add years to your life…and you will end up with fewer wrinkles, too!

Your Relationship with Yourself

What can you do to be the best you can be? The first step is to take an honest look at how you feel about yourself. Your feelings affect everything in your life. Do you have feelings of inadequacy that you just don't measure up to someone's expectations? Well, we're here to tell you that this is totally unacceptable. Think about this: there is nothing and no one in the entire universe like you. You are unique, one of a kind. No one has your brain, your eyes, your mouth, or your hair. No one has your DNA. There is only one human being in this vast universe that is you. Wow!

You need to see and believe in the wonderful, special person you are. Think of all the positive, thoughtful things you have done. Think of the kindness, joy, and laughter you bring to those around you. If you feel inadequate or inferior to others, where did those feelings come from? Try to determine the origin of your feelings and then set the record straight with yourself—whoever made you feel that way was wrong. It was about them, not about you!

Each and every day, moment-by-moment, you are indeed a special being. Remember this because when you see and feel how wonderful you are, the possibilities will lead you in the direction of greatness.

> *Remember, happiness doesn't depend upon who you are or what you have; it depends solely upon what you think.*
>
> —Dale Carnegie

Where Are You?

The first step in understanding ourselves is to give serious thought to where we are today, right here, right now. This is your starting point. Recognizing where we are helps us understand who we are. The choices you have made and the choices you want to make reveal who you are. One of the most important tools we have is the power to choose. What choices are you making, and where will they take you? Making wise choices is a skill set we need to develop and refine continually.

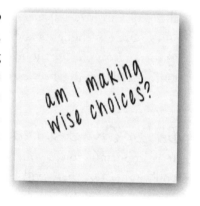

Your mind-set and attitude are important components of where you want to be. Sometimes we feel like we have all the education and the knowledge we need in our professional and personal lives, but for some reason, we're not moving ahead. Something is missing, and that causes a feeling of unrest. That is life telling us that it is time for change.

Do What You Can

It's impossible to know it all or be able to do it all. The key is to know what *you can* do and then do it. What *you can* do…you do! You're successful if you're doing the best you can with the skills you have. Sometimes the most courageous thing *you can* do is to get up and start all over again. There are times when that alone takes real strength and determination.

Don't waste your time wishing you could do things that someone else does. Instead, think of what *you can* do…what you want to do… what you like to do…and use what you already know. You don't need to be stronger. You don't need to have greater ability. You don't need to be anything but who you are. What we all need is to love ourselves, to be ourselves, and to use our thoughts and actions to move us forward on our life's journey. We start our journey today with who we are.

Be Your Own Best Friend

It is important to be your own best friend, because sometimes that's all you've got. Yes, there will be outside influences, other people who might not be on the same page as you are in your growth. They may not understand your need for personal focus and your search to find the "me" in all of your personal evaluation and self-reflection. They may feel threatened that you want to change and grow. Yes, we do need other people in our lives, and indeed part of who we are is the culmination of other people's influences. But it is up to you to distinguish the positive influences from the negative and leave the toxic people behind you as you move forward on your journey.

Why not be your own best friend? You're going to be with yourself for a lifetime. It is better to learn to love yourself sooner rather than later. This book is about you and how to embrace the best of who you are and what *you can* be.

You are the only person you can control or count on to be there at all times. You are always there, even in those times when you wish you could get as far away from yourself as possible. You are always there for yourself, through the bad times and the most joyful of times. You are always there, and always will be. This is why it is so important to be your own best friend. Unfortunately, sometimes we forget this most important fact.

Promise me you'll always remember...
you're braver than you believe and stronger
than you seem and smarter than you think.
—Christopher Robin to Winnie the Pooh

We Must Change Before We Can Grow

Oh, no! Not change! Change is uncomfortable for most of us. If change is something that's outside of your comfort zone, know that you are not alone. When life says, "It's time to grow," we have to let go of some of the old in order to make room for the new. When we need to grow, we need to change. The need for growth becomes a motivating force.

We all have had those feelings that we just won't let go. You know those thoughts that just keep gnawing at you. They are our "I wonder what if I…" thoughts, or maybe we should call these our "I wish I would of, could of, or should of…" thoughts. They might take the form of "I would love to…" or "Wouldn't that be interesting…" or "I have always wanted to try that…" Pay attention to the thoughts that you think over and over, the thoughts that keep coming back. No matter how many times you have just shrugged them off, your mind keeps returning to them.

Let's say that you have been thinking about taking up a new sport, or taking classes to improve your game. Maybe you have wanted to take an art class, attend a seminar, or learn to dance. Perhaps your thoughts keep going back to a family vacation that your mind dreams about. Maybe it is a class that would help you move up in your career. Maybe it is time for you to find a new career. Whatever thoughts your imagination keeps bringing to the front of your mind, pay attention to these. They are there because it's time for a change. Remind yourself that to grow, we have to let go. Change may very well be your best friend.

To really succeed, and to feel great all the time, it is important to learn to live with the right attitude—a willingness to move beyond what you know, to accept something even better. Having the right mind-set and attitude requires change, and the rewards can be extraordinary.

> *A lot of times people look at the negative*
> *side of what they feel they can't do.*
>
> *I always look on the positive side of what I can do.*
>
> —Chuck Norris

Change I Can't to I Can!

Who are you? What do you want to do? Where do you want to go? Be sure you're going in the direction that will lead you to your ultimate goals. You have chosen to invest some time to work *on* your life instead of *in* your life. This will enable you to be proactive in your approach to things rather than reactive. This allows time to plan and to take charge, one topic at a time.

For example, what if you feel like your days are out of control? You feel that your time is not being well spent? At the end of the day, are you sure you have actually accomplished anything that you set out to do? This can be a common reflection for many of us. The solution is to have a plan that puts you in charge of your day and how you spend your time.

A simple time-blocking method could be all that you need. For example, make a conscious choice about when you receive or return calls and e-mails. This works on a personal and professional basis.

Change your voice mail message or e-mail reply to indicate the specific time that you will be returning calls or e-mails. This gives you the control and needed personal time. You now have an opportunity to complete a project without interruption and to get the things done that you set out to do. Think about this for a moment and realize that there are so many interruptions that we deal with on a daily basis. We are more productive when we are not randomly derailed and refocused. This requires a plan for being in charge of your time and of your schedule.

Think of the habits you must change, and replace those addictions with positive, productive use of your time. You get to be the person in charge. In reality, intrusion and disruption can be avoided, and it is OK to take control of your day. Getting organized and taking charge of your time is a critical first step. Controlling your schedule and your calendar is the foundation of the planning process. Once you become proactive with your time, you become more organized and better prepared to start your new journey. What you do and when you choose to do it is simply up to you!

Your New Journey

Start this journey with a map so that you keep moving in the right direction to achieve your maximum potential. You're on a new journey. Define what you expect to accomplish by taking a little time out for yourself. In this "Who am I?" evaluation, you are searching for the "I" that makes you "you."

Ask yourself, "What is it that I love?" and "What do I love about me?" Take some time to really look at your life and how you are living it. How do you see your world, and what would you change? If you could do anything in the world, what would it be? Let your imagination soar! What would make you get up each day, knowing that your life was filled with excitement and that you are ready for the adventure ahead? These questions will define what your life can become.

Start by looking at your strengths. List the best of who you are and what you can be. What do you value most about yourself? Why do you feel this way? List what you are good at. What are the things you like to do? What makes you happy? Ask your friends for their input. Now give yourself permission to do more of the things that fall under the category of fun, likes, and strengths.

What's Special about Me?

You are defined by the positive things that are you. The three questions below focus on your strengths. The idea is to help you see that unique, special person you are. It's your list, so be honest. This is not the time to be humble or modest. Be your own best friend or ask your friends, and list all the wonderful things that are uniquely wonderful about you. Don't compare yourself to anyone else. Don't be judgmental. Don't sell yourself short. Where do you shine?

What gifts do you bring to the table? Let's just work on making this an incredibly long list.

Why I Am Special:

1. What are my strengths? What am I good at?

_____

_____

_____

2. What do I like to do? How does this make me feel?

_____

_____

_____

3. What do I dream about doing? How does *this* make me feel?

_____

_____

_____

You've just got to be yourself and decide where
you're at and where you want to be.

—Marshall Faulk

Three

Formulate Your Thinking

All that you are is a result of all that you have thought.

—Buddha

Thoughts Are Things

Think smart, act smart, and be smart. Our thoughts shape our world. You are what you think, and what you think determines who you are. You are creating your life and the world you live in. Perception is everything. Thoughts are things. What are you thinking?

It has been said that thousands of thoughts go through each person's mind each and every day, over and over and over. Most are negative. Let's change that!

Focus On the Lesson Learned

An example of negative thinking is regret. We regret our mistakes, although mistakes tend to be more memorable than successes. They can, and do, foster regret. We learn from our mistakes as well as from our successes. However, we do learn from these actions and their resulting outcomes. We all have regrets, but living with regret is unproductive and has no place in our lives. We have to be responsible for our negative actions. That's a given.

We must become aware of our negative thinking because it is nonproductive and unhealthy. Whether we regret things we did do or things we did not do, they are all in the past. Make amends and move on. Let them go.

In fact, by changing your focus from the negative aspects of an experience to what you have learned from the experience, you are changing the experience to a positive outcome. Now you are thinking and seeing yourself in a more positive light. This is a healthy and productive way to live your life.

Positive Personal Space

Thoughts are things. When you change your thoughts, your new thinking will change your life. It's not easy, but it is worth the effort. Don't sabotage yourself with negative energy. Thoughts and self-talk are where all the negativity begins. If you find yourself harboring a negative thought or fixating on something negative someone has said to or about you, just say, "Don't put that in my space." Your personal space should be a positive place.

The concept of protecting your personal space is very important. It is up to you. It's your space, and you are responsible for who and what you allow into your personal space. Steer clear of negativity, as it only breeds more negativity and has no positive outcome. Allowing and participating in negative thoughts and actions is exhausting and creates a negative spiral we want to avoid. Instead, surround yourself with positive energy, people, places, and things, as this is critical. Positive energy is important and it cannot and should not be underestimated.

Ask yourself, "What thoughts do I need to change to have the most positive image of myself?" Your thinking has a direct effect on how you act and feel. You become what you think. You owe it to yourself to be aware of what you are thinking. You are in control of your thoughts, so why not change your thoughts and think positive? Keep thinking *I can, I can, I can*. That becomes your self-talk. By changing your thoughts, you can change your life. It requires effort and practice, but the end result is worth it.

> *How we think shows through in how we act. Attitudes are mirrors of the mind. They reflect thinking.*
> —David Joseph Schwartz

The Rule Is as Simple as the ABCs

Changing negative thoughts to positive thoughts can be as simple as the ABCs:

A. Attitude
B. Belief
C. Courage

> *Attitude is a little thing that makes a big difference.*
> —Winston Churchill

A Is for Attitude: Change a Negative Attitude to a Positive One

What is your attitude? Do you feel that you have everything you need to succeed: knowledge, contacts, and skills? These are all important, but they will only take you part of the way. To achieve your highest potential, you must have the right attitude. You will truly succeed only if you develop a positive attitude.

The way to develop a positive attitude is to your thoughts. It is so important to change your thoughts, because in doing so you will change your life. Having a positive attitude will change the way you look at life. Your attitude affects the health of your mind, body, and emotions.

Start today by making better decisions and smarter choices. Engage in regular mind, body, and spirit exercises that will increase and nurture a positive attitude. When your mind, body, and spirit are in a positive space, you are functioning from a position of strength and your decision-making skills are crisp and clear, and will result in smarter and better choices.

Here is an exercise to get you started:

List three positive attitudes you tend to exhibit:

1. _____

2. _____

3. _____

Now list three negative attitudes you tend to exhibit and would like to change:

1. _____

2. _____

3. _____

Pay close attention to when you are thinking negative thoughts or exhibiting negative attitudes. At the moment you realize you are doing it, find a way to stop and change the negative thought to a positive one. For example, if you find yourself thinking, "I will not get this promotion," think instead of the reasons you should be selected for the promotion. Go over those positive thoughts in your mind as often as you can. Believe them. Change your attitude by changing your thoughts. This will change your life.

Try this trick: wear a rubber band around your wrist, and when you think a negative thought, snap the rubber band. "Ouch!" This will remind you to direct your thoughts to be positive and productive.

> *If you can dream it, you can do it. Always remember that*
> *this whole thing was started with a dream and a mouse.*
> —Walt E. Disney

B Is for Belief: Nurture the Belief That Anything Is Possible

Always believe in yourself. Be the person you want to be. If you want to see something happen in your life, you must first entertain the belief that your something is possible. To accomplish anything, you must believe that it *can* be true for you. Feel it in your heart, your soul, and your body. Feel it in every fiber of your being. Always be a warrior for yourself.

When your objective is to make a change in your life, one of the first questions you will need to ask yourself is: "How will taking this new path make me feel?" "Will it make me feel happy, respected, and peaceful?" "Will the journey be fulfilling?" "Is this a realistic journey?" For our wishes and dreams to come true, we have to first believe they are possible for us. You have to feel it, and believe it, before you can see it. Let this be true for you, and not the other way around. Think about this for a moment.

If you set out on a new journey but you don't believe in the changes that you want to make, if you can't feel it in your heart, then all the wishing in the world will not help you achieve your destination. Can you see yourself succeeding? Can you feel yourself in this new role? If not, your goal will not be achieved.

Faith is to believe what you do not see;
the reward of this faith is to see what you believe.

—Saint Augustine

I'll See It, When I Believe It

That old saying, "I'll believe it when I see it," is backward. You have to believe before *you can* see it, not the other way around. When you change it around and believe it first, you're as good as there. Just see it for yourself, believe that you are there, feel it, and the goal will be achieved. Ask yourself, "Do I really believe that this is possible for me?" "Do I believe I can do this?" And finally ask, "How does this make me feel?" You have to feel good about your new goal.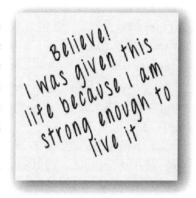

Give yourself permission to be the person you are meant to be. You have to want it so badly that nothing else feels right. Have the kind of faith you had as a child, when you believed in magic. There was never any doubt. You just knew. When was the last time your belief system felt like that? Embrace your childlike wonder to find that "I believe" place once again.

When you set out to accomplish a goal, you need to envision the goal completed. If you can't see and feel the goal, your goal will not be achieved. How you feel affects your thinking. How and what you feel about yourself can and will have an effect on everything and everyone around you. Every day thousands upon thousands of thoughts go through our minds, and many of them are erroneous. Nonetheless, we think them. They can keep us up at night and they can stop us from being the best we can be, but only if we let them.

Believe in Yourself

How many times have you heard, "Don't make the same mistakes I made. Instead, learn from them and make new ones on your own. Grow from them." Our motto is, "Believe in yourself and always look for the positive." Don't be vulnerable to self-doubt.

If you have feelings of inadequacy or you just don't feel quite good enough… guess what? You need to *change that channel* because negative thinking is totally unacceptable. We typically don't give a second thought to the amazement of how we we're created. But we are complex creatures. Just think about what has to happen within our bodies just to blink, to raise our hand, to walk and talk.

Take some time right now to concentrate, to really think about this amazing vessel that you are, and if you dare to think you're not worthy, this is a good time to shift your thoughts to a positive place. See only the miracle that is you, and validate that by identifying the positive parts of you!

Give some thought to the following questions. Your answers will clarify the path you will want to follow and what action you will need to take.

What are three things you believe, feel, and can visualize as a new path that you want for yourself?

1. _____

2. _____

3. _____

If you push through that feeling of being scared, that
feeling of taking risk, really amazing things can happen

—Marissa Mayer, President and CEO of Yahoo

C Is for Courage: Step Outside Your Comfort Zone

It takes courage to believe in yourself, to make choices, and to face challenges. Develop the courage to do just that, and it will build your confidence. Sometimes the most courageous thing you can do is to just get up the next morning and start all over again. There are days when this takes real courage. We have all been there at some time in our lives.

"Courage is fear that has said its prayers"

—Karle Wilson Baker

Now is the time to start thinking about taking a new path. The time to act is now, so let's work with what we have. Let's get started and use the precious time we have to accomplish the most we can. Every minute you have is a gift for you to use and to invest in yourself. You cannot see any returns unless you start.

To accomplish anything, what do you need to do? What is necessary for your journey to begin? Start by using the resources you already have to work with. Be yourself. The rest will come.

"Bloom where you are planted."

—Mary Engelbreit

You are successful if you're doing the best you can with what you have. Your dream is here! The time to act is now! Start living your dream using the tools you have.

List three accomplishments that required your *courage*:

1. _____

2. _____

3. _____

> *Success is piece of mind which is a direct result of self-*
> *satisfaction in knowing you did your best to become*
> *the best that you are capable of becoming.*

> —John Wooden

Four

Get Back to Basics

In times of crisis, whether wild fires or smoldering stress,
the first thing to do is go back to basics…
am I eating right, am I getting enough sleep,
am I getting some physical and mental exercise every day?

—Edward Albert

The Three Systems of the Human Body:

1. Physical - *Your Body*
2. Intellectual – *Your Mind*
3. Psychological – *Your Emotions*

When you don't know what to do, get back to basics. Focus on nurturing the three systems of the human body: physical, intellectual, and psychological. In other words, take care of your body, mind, and emotions.

To keep the body in good health is a duty…otherwise, we
shall not be able to keep our mind strong and clear.

—Buddha

Physical – Your Body

The most basic of all the body's components is the physical aspect, so let's start here. Have you been wanting to join a gym, enroll in a weight-loss program, take a class in healthy cooking, or start walking regularly with a friend? There are so many resources and a lot of support that you can easily tap into.

Do what you know you need to do—no excuses. Take action! Read, research, and reach out. You must own the responsibility for taking care of your own body. You can start by listening to your body and paying attention. Are you getting enough water, healthy food, and exercise? We often feel like we don't have the time to exercise. But let us not become so distracted that we forget that our physical well-being should be a major priority. Don't forget your regular medical exams, and talk to your doctor about a course of action to stay healthy.

One simple action you can take to make yourself feel and look better is to watch your posture. This is so very important. Keep your head up and your shoulders back. Move with attitude. You are successful, so look the part! Do what you need to do daily to stay physically healthy, within your ability to do so. Take it one day at a time, moment by moment. Do something, anything… just move! Tell yourself, "*I can* do this."

Remember, *it's as simple as 1-2-3!* Three of the most important things we can do for our physical health cost nothing: wake, walk, and water.

Your physical goal might be to pay more attention to the three Ws:

1. *Wake:* Get up an hour earlier and get your exercise done for the day, meditate, write in your journal, or appreciate a cup of coffee or tea in the quiet of the morning.

2. *Walk:* Get in some free exercise by yourself, with your dog, with a neighbor, with family members, or with a friend. It's great for your physical and emotional well-being.

3. *Water:* Our bodies need plenty of water.

List three actions *you can* and *will* do to improve your physical health:

1. _____

2. _____

3. _____

A calm mind brings inner strength and self-confidence.

—Dalai Lama

Intellectual – Your Mind:

In the world of technology, we are always reminded, "Garbage in, garbage out." If you enter incorrect data into the computer, it will compute meaningless results. Our minds are similar. What you think will show up in your outcome. You have to give your mind the right orders through your thoughts and the visualized image you project of yourself in your mind.

Keep your mind active. Do what you need to do. Take classes, either online or in person. Always learn something new. Read a book that will give your mind food for thought, that will make you laugh or teach you something new. Benefit from the constructive knowledge of others, and allow their positive thoughts into

Knowledge is power

your personal space. Listen to positive audio programs, lectures, and connected learning resources.

Knowledge is the one thing that no one can take away from you. The more you learn, the more you know, and the more you know, the more you learn. "Life is for learning, and learning is life."

We are creative beings. Everything that exists has been created because someone had enough imagination to ask, "Why?" or "Why not?" Our minds need to be active. We are never finished learning, and that's a good thing. Every day is a lesson. Feed your mind every day, because a healthy mind has the capacity to grow and be more, regardless of age.

The more we learn, the more we realize how little we know. The universe is amazing, just as we are. We have a basic need to expand our mental intellect, to strive to be as knowledgeable as possible. Increasing your knowledge is a good goal and will be useful in living your life to the fullest.

> *I really had a lot of dreams when I was a kid, and I think*
> *a great deal of that grew out of the fact that I had a chance*
> *to read a lot.*
>
> —Bill Gates

List three actions *you can* take now to learn something new:

1. _____

2. _____

3. _____

Now list three actions *you can* take now to create a positive mind-set:

1. _____

2. _____

3. _____

Become the change you want to see...those are words I live by.

—Oprah Winfrey

Psychological – Your Emotions:

Set some rules for keeping your emotions in check. You are taking some giant steps on this new path that you have chosen. Remember when we talked about opposition and how it rears its head every time you make a decision to change? Understand what is triggering any emotional response you may have so you will know how to deal with it.

I have learned over the years that when one's
mind is made up, this diminishes fear.

—Rosa Parks

Fear of the Unknown

Remember the first time you faced something new that made you uncomfortable or scared? For example, the first time you dove off a diving board into a pool. What were you afraid of? Being hurt? Looking like a fool? Those were the things you said in your head, but your real fear was the unknown—the unknown, beginning from when your feet left the board to when your head went under the water.

You knew what it was like to walk, so walking out on the board was not the emotional part. Also, you knew what it was like to hold your breath, go underwater, come back up, catch a new breath of air, and swim to the side of the pool. These were the "knowns." There were no butterflies in the pit of your stomach over this. But it's the "unknowns" that took control of your emotions. In fact, there were some who would not overcome the fear of the unknown and would back themselves off that board without diving or perhaps without ever having ventured onto the board in the first place.

The best way to control *fear of the unknown* is to visualize the complete process of knowns and unknowns in a situation together. As in the example above; visualize approaching the board, walking to its front edge, making sure it's safe to dive, feeling your feet leave the board, and holding your breath just as you are about to enter the water. Then see yourself coming back up, and as your head clears the water, you taking another breath. Then visualize yourself working your way to the side of the pool. You have just made an "unknown" into a "known," and it may have only taken a few moments to do.

We are not saying that you won't still have butterflies, but you will learn to control those feelings. The more you practice visualizing, the more control you will have over the fear.

Practice visualizing before meeting with a new client, asking the boss for a raise, or asking someone out for the first time, and so on. We are not saying that you won't get a "no" in response; we are saying that this method will help you control the *fear of the unknown.*

Remember, we are not saying that you should not listen to your fears. Nature has put them in us for very good reasons! Some fears are real, but some are only in our imagination. Imagined fears hinder growth and impede your success. Eliminate those that are false, and identify and control those that are real.

*Be patient and persistent. Life is not so much
what you accomplish, as what you overcome*

—Robin Roberts, ABC's Good Morning America

What Do You Think?

This is a question that is frequently asked. In actuality, a more appropriate question often is, "How do you feel?" These *are* very different questions. When we are asked to "think" about an answer that is an entirely different process than asking us how we "feel" about something.

Thinking is analytical. When we analyze, it takes more time and involves comparisons, quantitative reasoning, and a check to make sure that the answer is logical and resonates as reasonable.

In contrast, to ask someone how they "feel" about something requires only to check in on one's emotion. We often are looking for input on how the other person feels, more so than their analysis. We want more of their initial reaction, to the topic at hand.

The next time you are tempted to ask someone what he or she thinks, perhaps you are actually more interested in how they feel. The answer could be as simple as, "Better and better every day," which can put us in control of our positive emotional space and get us ready for personal growth.

"It Is What It Is"

We have all heard the saying, "It is what it is." Most of the time this saying comes as a negative response that aims to change the perception, or deflect from the behavior of one's actions or questions that they do not want to own. Imagine the ramification that a negative attitude has on you and others. The reality is that no one wants or needs negative behavior. Watch how negative body language will show through on someone who is angry or depressed. Ask yourself, how did that make you feel? Remember, strive to keep your personal space positive, joyful, and productive. The end result is a culmination of what your psychological experience will be.

Protect your personal space and let your positive personality influence your personal interactions. The next time you hear, "It is what it is," your reply can be, "But it will become what I make it."

If you correct your mind, the rest of your life will fall into place.
—Lao Tzu

List three things that you feel good about in your life:

1. _____

2. _____

3. _____

List three ways that you are getting "better and better" every day:

1. _____

2. _____

3. _____

List three accomplishments that required your *courage*:

1. _____

2. _____

3. _____

Five

Your Core Belief and Intuition

Your time is limited, so don't waste it living someone else's life. Don't be trapped by dogma—which is living with the results of other people's thinking. Don't let the noise of others' opinions drown out your own inner voice. And most important, have the courage to follow your intuition.

—Steve Jobs

Core Belief

Your core belief is the highest degree of what you value. What you accept as true, whether it's a firm conviction, a trust, or a confidence, that is your core belief. It's that quiet voice you hear, letting you know when something does not align with what you believe in. Follow your inner voice; believe that it is your core belief speaking to you. Maybe you call it intuition or your gut feeling. Your core beliefs work in tandem with your intuition.

List three of your core beliefs:

1. _____

2. _____

3. _____

Intuition

Trust your intuition. Learn to rely on your intuition because it is the sum of all of your experiences and events that have contributed to the making of you. Pay close attention to your intuition, your gut feelings, your inner voice. The best answer always seems to be the one that feels right. Now, if you have any questions or doubts, you know to wait. Because when we have ignored our intuition, the situation has never worked out to be the best solution or action to take. Give this some thought, because we bet it works the same for you.

> *Some people say there's nothing new under the sun. I still think that there's room to create, and intuition doesn't necessarily come from under this sun, it comes from within.*
>
> —Pharrell Williams

List three examples of when you trusted your intuition:

1. _____

2. _____

3. _____

Living a Life Based on Positive Values

Your positive values result from a clear understanding of what you accept as true about
yourself and are demonstrated in the way you
live your life. Living a life based on values
involves having the confidence in the course of
action you take in any given situation. Many
people have their basic core values centered on
the Golden Rule, which inspires to treat others
as you would like to be treated.

When our core values are clear, it helps our decision-making. Living a life
based on positive values will accomplish positive results and direct us on the
right path. Goals based on a value system inspire us to put in the hard work
required to attain them. Because they challenge us, they keep our attention
long enough to accomplish them.

> *"It is curious that physical courage be so common*
> *in the world and moral courage so rare.*
>
> —Mark Twain

What are three of your positive values?

1. _____

2. _____

3. _____

> *The measure of who we are is what we do with what we have.*
>
> —Vince Lombardi

Six

Three Ts That Impact

If you can't fly, then run. If you can't run, then walk.
If you can't walk, then crawl. But whatever you do,
you have to keep moving forward.

—Martin Luther King, Jr.

In Every I Can't, There Is an I Can

Let's take the T out of *can't* and focus on *I can*. The following things impact our actions and activities to a great extent, and they all begin with the letter T: *time*, *temperament*, and *tenacity*.

1. Time

Time is one of our most valued assets. We can't make more of it, and we can't get it back. Once it's gone, it is gone forever. Be courageous. Don't waste your time wishing you could do things. Instead, think of what *you can* do… what you need to do…and do it, one step at a time. Sometimes you just have to get through it minute by minute, but minutes add up to

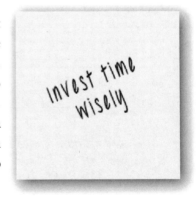

Invest time wisely

hours, hours add up to days, days become years, and years become a lifetime. How precious is your time?

We can do nothing to change something that happened five minutes ago, much less years ago. Yet we beat ourselves up over and over again, reliving the past. We should not waste our most valuable asset on things that cannot be changed. What's in the past is in the past; leave it there and move on. We are the product of our past, but it does not define us.

We can control ourselves going forward; that's why our eyes are at the front of our heads, not at the back. We need to focus forward and move on. Our present actions will influence and determine our future. What we do today will determine tomorrow's outcome. Your actions will set the groundwork for your future.

Life is what happens when we are busy making other plans.

—John Lennon

List three positive investments of your time that *you can* start making:

1. _____

2. _____

3. _____

At the end of your life, you will never regret not having
passed one more test, not winning one more verdict
or not closing one more deal. You will regret time not
spent with a husband, a friend, a child, or parent.

—Barbara Bush

2. Temperament

How are you living your life? Do you live it with excitement and enthusiasm? *You can*, you know; it just takes practice. Start each and every day by living with an attitude of gratitude. First thing each and every morning when you get out of bed, put one foot down and say, "Thank," then put the other foot down and say "you." In the evening as you climb into bed, again say, "Thank you." A grateful attitude that demonstrates appreciation and kindness will bring an abundance of joy into your life. Try it—you'll like it.

> *An intense temperament has convinced me to teach not only from books but from what we have learned from experience.*
>
> —Kay Redfield Jamison

We All Want to Be Appreciated

Some things are best valued when we give them away…like a smile. As we said before, a smile is contagious, but not like the measles; a smile is a good, good thing. As an example, at the office, I would get on the elevator, and for seventeen floors, I'd put a smile on my face and see how many other people I could "pass it on" to. Most people would take a breath and then respond in kind. I can't help but think that getting a smile, and giving a smile on the elevator ride, started their day off on a positive way. I know it did mine.

Sharing a smile is fun and easy to do. Try it sometime. It won't always be easy to smile, feel appreciation, and say "thank you." It may take some discipline to do those things when life isn't going well. But those are the times when it's more important than ever to have a pleasant, easygoing temperament. It's alright if you don't get a smile "right back at you"; those are the people that most likely need your smile the most. So smile away, because it makes for a happy heart.

> *Just as we develop our physical muscles through overcoming opposition – such as lifting weights - we develop our character muscles by overcoming challenges and adversity.*
>
> —Stephen Covey

Opposition

It might seem that making such an important change in your life, even in the face of adversity, might bring about instant and consistent rewards. That isn't the case, unfortunately. Our experience has shown that once you have made a commitment to change, there will be an up-and-down effect, a push and pull that happens once your mind is focused and you decide to make some changes. Be aware that this is natural and normal. You may experience opposition to some of your decisions. Opposition can rear its little head and cause you to doubt your own judgment. Recognize it for what it is, and move on. This may be the universe checking in on you to see how important this new change is to you. Don't let opposition be more than a small speed bump. Remember, you are in control.

Any time we make a decision to make, change, or break a habit, there is a natural opposition that takes place within each and every one of us. Our minds play a game on us to prevent us from making a change or moving forward. It's like the law of gravity: what goes up, must come down. Be aware that this opposition is a normal function of our minds, sort of the way we naturally resist change. This opposition to change is a normal and natural occurrence that happens to all of us once we make a decision to change.

Opposition can appear in the following forms:

- pessimism
- procrastination
- resistance
- negative thoughts, actions, and attitude
- feelings of inadequacy or incompetence
- antagonism/toxic people
- criticism
- disapproval
- fear
- pity parties/people feeling sorry for themselves
- the "poor little me" syndrome

You can fight opposition by giving yourself permission to:

- be confident
- be optimistic
- live with enthusiasm and excitement
- be creative, outrageous, and imaginative
- understand that change is necessary
- stay focused and be cheerful, calm, and confident
- trust your intuition and have faith
- know that you are valued
- have a strength of purpose
- know that your dreams can come true

> *There is no personal charm so great as the*
> *charm of a cheerful temperament.*
>
> —Henry Van Dyke

List three things *you can* do to improve your temperament:

1. _____

2. _____

3. _____

> *I've missed more than nine thousand shots in my career.*
> *I've lost almost three hundred games. Twenty-six times*
> *I've been trusted to take the game-winning shot and missed.*
> *I have failed over and over again in my*
> *life. And that is why I succeed.*
>
> —Michael Jordan

3. Tenacity

We define tenacity as determination. It is the unshakable commitment you must have to succeed. Tenacity will dictate how you will handle life's challenges. Are you willing to get up and try, and try, and try again? It is that all-or-nothing attitude that will move you forward with the dogged pursuit of a committed decision. When you are tenacious, you possess a "never give up" attitude, and you feel like you can accomplish anything. It is the consistent confidence to keep on keeping on, to never give up.

Tenacity can take the following forms:

- confidence
- an attitude of "there are no problems, only solutions"
- determination and commitment of purpose
- intention/a resolve to never give up
- unstoppable drive/stamina
- dedication to proceed with a plan
- effort, where action speaks volumes
- to live with joy, kindness, and love
- dedication to the goal
- a belief that there are endless possibilities

Tenacity is the "I can" attitude. Tell yourself, "Yes, I can," and give yourself permission to:

- dream
- be persistent
- be creative
- be bold
- be steadfast
- understand that the journey will be emotional
- go forward with dogged pursuit
- trust and know that you are worth it

- have strength of purpose
- know that *I can*

Again, in every *I can't* is an *I can.* Let's take the *T* out of *can't* and focus on what *you can* do.

List three areas of your life in which *you can* exhibit more tenacity:

1. _____

2. _____

3. _____

Do not follow where the pathway leads.
Go instead where there is no path and leave a trail.
—Unknown

Seven

Think Smart, Act Smart, Be Smart

What lies behind us and what lies before us
are tiny matters compared to what lies within us.

—Ralph Waldo Emerson

The Process: Your Path, Your Journey

The job of living life is a journey. Your journey has a path and a process in and of itself. Your journey will have purpose, and it will also have struggles. You will always meet obstacles on the road to your answers. Opposition unfolds, but one must remain undaunted, because obstacles are a part of life.

Now is the time to set your course. With your mind ready, make the commitment and put your action plan into place. Set your mind to always focus forward. As in any journey, continue to follow your map, pivoting and turning as obstacles appear. Many times these obstacles will point in a direction that lead to excellent opportunities. This is not always apparent, but continue with your journey, and continue to focus forward.

So here you are, face to face with yourself. The next step is to develop a process that will help you solidify your dream. Continue on, with trust and faith that you are on the right path. You have evaluated yourself and developed some strategies. Your course is set, your mind is ready, and your commitment is made. You are ready to put an action plan into place. Always focus forward, because the purpose of this journey is to discover the best you possible.

The Process Is as Simple as 1-2-3

Although the process is *as simple as 1-2-3*, it's not easy. In fact, change is difficult, and whatever your intention is, it will require change. We often resist change because with change comes opposition. Just realize that this resistance to change is a natural process of life whenever we set out to make changes in our life's journey. Everyone experiences some opposition when they decide to make changes. It's as natural as gravity.

Maybe resistance is nature's way of asking: How important is this change to you? Is your dream strong enough that you will forge through any resistance and move forward, no matter what? Are you willing to take a new path and follow you dreams? We believe that if you do, your hopes and dreams will be delivered to you.

Again, it sounds simple, but it's not easy. If change were easy, everyone would be doing something to change, and we all know that's not happening. Setting goals is life changing. If your purpose has worth, then aim your ambition high because your effort will result in reaching the targeted objectives you set. Remember, you are worth it!

If you correct your mind, the rest of your life will fall into place.

—Lao Tzu

The Three-Step Plan

To accomplish your goals in the most effective and efficient way possible, consider this three-step process. Here are the details of this plan.

1. Think Smart

Stop and think before taking action. Sometimes the old must make way and move over for the new. Really think about the "why" behind what you're doing. Give yourself permission to grow and let go.

Strategy

It is not always easy to be positive in attitude, belief, and action. Recognize that your self-talk becomes your personal image, since your thoughts influence the perceived image you have of yourself. When working on your self-image, stay positive and upbeat. Instead of focusing on negatives, validate your positive thoughts. Observe yourself without placing judgment on yourself. Know what you are good at and what you like to do. Always encourage others, and seek encouragement for yourself.

If you find that sometimes it is difficult to be positive and upbeat, friends can help. Call a friend who is a positive person, or think of a person you really enjoy talking to, someone who makes you feel good about yourself or who is just fun to be around. Set a date and spend time with that person. Try to do this within a few days. Even if it's just for a moment or two, or maybe only a phone call, it will help. Once you have spent time with that person, thank him or her. Write a thank-you note to show your appreciation for that person's positive presence in your day. Typically, a positive person is happy to be called on in the future, if the need arises, for another quick dose of positive energy.

Actions to Take

- Radiate enthusiasm.
- Start to plan for personal growth through setting goals.
- Have confidence when moving forward.
- Start small. Small is where big begins. Small ideas will lead to bigger ideas.
- Prioritize. You cannot do everything at one time.
- Find a good mentor who has accomplished something you would like to set as your goal.

- Listen and learn from your mentor, and be open to his or her input.
- Think gracious thoughts.
- Have a sincere attitude of gratitude.
- Don't forget to have fun.

To think is to practice brain chemistry.

—Deepak Chopra

List three thoughts about your personal growth plan to "think smart":

1. _____

2. _____

3. _____

The most difficult thing is the decision to act, the rest is
merely tenacity. The fears are paper tigers. You can do
anything you decide to do. You can act to change and control
your life; and the procedure, the process is our reward.

—Amelia Earhart

2. Act Smart

It is important to understand why you behave in certain ways and, if necessary, to modify how you act. Be in charge of your actions. It is up to you to act smart.

Strategy

An attitude of action must include an effective decision-making process. It's up to you. No decision is a decision. Only *you can* decide to take action. Don't be afraid, and don't let fear stop you. Approach your process as you would a recipe: take it step by step, one step at a time, each one in succession. Take action steps that are not too complicated to remember. Work the plan. Schedule your activities and allow enough time to complete each one without rushing. Use only one calendar that includes time for family, career, personal activities, and social opportunities. Have a positive attitude, and prepare an action plan to help you maintain it.

By implementing an action plan, you are in the driver's seat. Have a positive attitude and prepare an action plan to help you move forward. Budget your time, emotion, and focus.

When you need a break, physical activity is one of the best ways to promote emotional health. If you have been sitting for awhile, stand up and take a walk around the room or the neighborhood. Just get up and move. Stroll through the park. Greet your neighbors. Enjoy the weather, rain or shine. The plan is to change your surroundings, to get a different view, and to get your body moving. Open your eyes and focus on something else. See the world around you; feel the air around you. Have a deliberate intention to be present and to get a fresh perspective on your surroundings.

Actions to Take

- K.I.S.S: Keep it simple, silly.
- Stay in a position of strength.
- Trust in your skills and use them.
- How do your new actions make you feel?
- Remember that your attitude is your choice.
- Continue to learn: what *you can* do...you do!
- Use your knowledge as a steppingstone to new goals.
- If you take three steps forward and one step back, you're still two steps ahead.
- Have confidence, enthusiasm, determination, kindness, and purity of purpose.

- Spend your time wisely. Time is your friend and one of our most valuable assets.

You may never know what results come from your action.
But if you do nothing there will be no result.

—Mahatma Gandhi

List three thoughts about your progress and personal growth plan to "act smart":

1. _____

2. _____

3. _____

3. Be Smart

Be aware of your thoughts and actions, and of the signals you are sending. We need to understand why we behave as we do and stay in control of how we think, act, and are. By controlling the things we can control, such as our thoughts and our reaction to situations, we are thinking smart, we are acting smart and, because of our actions and thinking, we are smart.

Strategy

Intellectual and emotional input enters into our personal space continually. Be keenly aware of what you are reading, watching, and listening to. Be aware of the attitudes of the people you allow into your life. Seek to counter any negative input with positive influences. Schedule time in your day to fill yourself intellectually with constructive and encouraging messages. Choose to have your mind, body, and spirit move in the direction of positive thoughts, words, and actions. Develop your *I can* attitude. Remember that a celebration once you reach your destination will remind you that you have arrived and will emotionally reinforce your belief in your ability to accomplish a goal you set for yourself.

Actions to Take

- Believe in endless possibilities.
- Give yourself permission to grow and let go.
- Trust your intuition and let it support your beliefs.
- Actualize to realize by seeing your goal as if you were already there.
- Realize that we have no problems, just solutions we have not found yet.
- Ask yourself if you are proceeding with enthusiasm.
- Develop yourself, and rewards will follow.
- Don't forget to reward yourself.
- Encourage yourself and be your best friend.

List three thoughts about your personal growth plan to "be smart":

1. _____

2. _____

3. _____

Make each day your masterpiece.
—John Wooden

Questions for Self-Reflection

What are three positive *think smart* activities you currently do?

1. _____

2. _____

3. _____

What are three positive *act smart* activities you currently practice?

1. _____

2. _____

3. _____

What are three positive *be smart* activities you currently practice?

1. _____

2. _____

3. _____

What are three new activities you would like to add to your daily routine?

1. *Think smart:* _____

2. *Act smart:* _____

3. *Be smart:* _____

Eight

Act: Activities and Action

*When you revolutionize education, you're taking the very
mechanism of how people can be smarter and do new things,
and you're primping the pump for so many incredible things.*

—Bill Gates

Activities and Action

Now that we have talked about the importance of analyzing your strengths, thinking positive thoughts, and believing in yourself, it's time to participate in some activities and take some action to optimize our gifts and achieve as much as possible.

*"If you don't design your own life plan, chances
are you'll fall into someone else's plan. And guess
what they have planned for you? Not much."*

—Jim Rohn

Prepare to Plan

Setting a goal requires a personal commitment; it's a contract you make with yourself. As with any commitment, we have to put in the necessary effort for achievement to take place. Just setting the goal doesn't make it happen.

The development of a plan for your new life begins with getting prepared. Your goal setting plan should be an exciting adventure. Remember, we want to have fun and enjoy our journey. We don't want to get too overwhelmed, so let's keep it *as simple as 1-2-3*. Often, the good things are the simple things, and simple things start with simple goals. The key is to start.

As in any journey, we want to follow a plan. Here we will follow an activity plan that will serve as our guide to help keep us on the right path. Only you can take the necessary actions to improve your future. Yes, it is up to you!

Build a Business Plan for Your Life

In our work environment, we create business plans that outline specific actions and activities. We are judged by our performance in achieving the stated objectives and executing the actions and activities that led to the achievement of the stated plan. The job of life is like a business—we define our life's plan by setting goals and working diligently to achieve them.

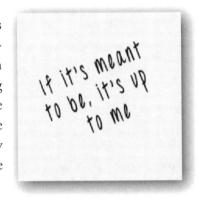

If it's meant to be, it's up to me

Your life is like running a business. You set goals, work toward them, review, revise, recalibrate, and keep going forward. Your life is the most important business you will ever have. Your life must have a plan and a purpose. Not having a plan is like waiting for an accident to happen. Why would we ever want to leave our destiny to chance? We are all going to end up somewhere, so we might as well choose what we want our lives to be. Make the choice and let your life's journey be defined with a clear map, a planned path, and a targeted destination.

> *"You cannot connect the dots looking forward; you can*
> *only connect them looking backward. So you have to*
> *trust that the dots will somehow connect in your future.*

*You have to trust in something—your gut, destiny,
life, karma, whatever. This approach has never let me
down, and it has made all the difference in my life.*

—Steve Jobs

Desire: Nature's Whisper

Intuition. It is called many things: "I have a gut feeling," "A voice in my head," "I just keep thinking about..." No matter how you say it, this is how our species communicates intuitive feeling to ourselves, almost as if nature itself were talking to us.

It is personal, private, and between you and nature. It's as if nature is whispering, "It's just you and me." So when your intuition, that gut feeling, places a desire in your mind and heart, maybe, just maybe, you should pay close attention to it. There is a reason for that desire. It may represent an important life lesson that you are meant to learn at this time in your life. Remember, your path is your life's journey.

If you could do anything, what would you do? Dare to dream. Shoot for the moon. The worst-case scenario is that you might settle for a star! Don't let the question of how it will get done limit the what of your dream. Your decisions, and the choices you make, will determine your destiny. Dreams and desires are not an all-or-nothing proposition, just as our daily life is not an all-or-nothing experience. Your desire is rarely an extreme undertaking. More often than not, the balance lies somewhere in between. Your starting point is the place that feels the most comfortable to you and therefore can serve as a good launching pad for the work ahead.

Take a Balanced Approach

Approach your desire for change with balance. Moderation is a good rule to gauge most of life's activities by, and it absolutely applies here. Our self-confidence should contain enough of a balance to face our objective bravely. Do not ever give into fear; it should never be powerful enough to stop you from making progress. The best way to keep fear away is to remember that it is an acronym for *False Expectations Appearing Real*. Thank you to the person who first came up with this acronym, because it puts fear in proper perspective for us. It is false, and we should identify it as such. We need to have the confidence and drive that are necessary to give ourselves permission to move right past any fear that we may have. We set an objective and take the necessary action to move forward with our desired changes. It's your life: follow your desire to achieve and accomplish any worthy goal for your life.

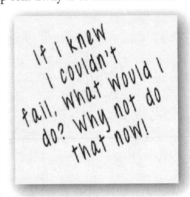

Proceed with Due Diligence

In law, due diligence means taking reasonable steps to satisfy a legal requirement, especially in buying or selling something. To proceed with due diligence as we strive to accomplish a goal means that when we set personal growth goals, we have some homework to do. Take a hard look at your thoughts about your goals. Scrutinize them for viability, importance, purpose, and relevance. Do your goals align with your core values? Do your goals blend with or adhere to your core belief system, or do they aim to achieve a goal that is outside of your core belief system? Everything must be congruent or your efforts will be met with conflict and disarray.

Check Your Attitude

A positive attitude is imperative and it defines what you will be able to accomplish. It is important to check in on your attitude regularly to make sure it reflects confidence, kindness, enthusiasm, belief, purpose, and gratitude.

Take Control of Your Self-Image

The only person you can control is yourself. Therefore, taking control of your self-image will cause your actions to come from a position of strength instead of a position of weakness. When we function from a position of strength, we keep fear and doubt on the sidelines and help ourselves stay in control.

Listen to yourself. It could determine your destiny

In this position, our actions and choices are always the most productive. A positive sense of self will influence how others see us and how we are received, and their opinion of us often influences how we feel about ourselves. It is a bit cyclical, as some of life is. It is sort of like the age-old question of which came first, the chicken or the egg? In this situation, we have both to work with: both the chicken and the egg simultaneously, not in a sequence.

It is the same way with the perception others have of our self-image and us—they are being formed at the same time. We cannot control the perception others have of us, but we can influence it. Don't compare yourself to anyone else. You are unique and one of a kind.

Having positive goals that you are actively working on gives you encouragement and a feeling of accomplishment, which, in turn, make you feel really good about yourself. That good feeling, which then manifests itself as confidence and enthusiasm, will shine through and have a positive effect that can bounce right back at you and motivate you to stay totally focused on your goals until an unflinching *I can* attitude is your result.

Focus on the Future, Not on the Past

Our goals help us stay focused on the things we want to accomplish. Goals help us stay present in the moment and to have a finger firmly on the pulse of what is real and happening right now. Working on goals helps us steer clear of regret, that feeling of sadness for things we did not do. The wishing, the should-a, could-a, would-a, has no place here. No one wants or needs it. Regret is a negative feeling and not a positive motivator.

Focus on what you have, what you have done, and what you plan to do, always moving forward. You cannot go back and relive the past, so spending any energy on regrets is a waste of time. Focus forward and continue moving toward your goal. You cannot do that by looking in the rearview mirror all the time. An occasional glance backward is sometimes worthwhile, as long as its purpose is to better understand the task at hand. But what will keep you moving is a forward focus.

> *Knowing is not enough; we must apply.*
> *Willing is not enough; we must do.*
>
> —Bruce Lee

Look at Problems as Opportunities

Problems are opportunities. If you encounter a problem, identify at least three possible solutions. Be prepared with these possible solutions before you utter a single word indicating that you have found a problem. Always be a solution finder, not a problem creator. This brings great value to yourself and others because this skill is a stretch for many people. It will also greatly influence your outlook on life and make your world and the world around you a happier place. Don't be hard on yourself. You are successful if you're doing the best you can with what you have.

In practice, as managers, whenever anyone brought a problem to us, we would ask for potential solutions at the same time. This accomplished all of the things referenced above. The individual who found the problem was now forced to the next step of finding the solution. Living in a world of solutions is a better place to live than in a world of problems. Finding solutions is not always easy and often requires deliberate intention to think outside the box. If solutions were so obvious, there would not be so many problems.

There are people (and we all have met more than a few) who seem to enjoy the fact that there is a problem and will stay in the world of the problem just as long as possible. Sometimes they can hang onto a problem for years and years. Stay clear from toxic people and their problems.

In the *I can* world, finding a problem is not the end, it is the beginning. In the *I can* world, we are problem solvers, not problem owners.

Control and Influence

Let's keep our job of life in proper perspective. There are only three possible scenarios in any situation:

- *You can* **control** it (whatever *it* is). The only person you can control is yourself.
- *You can* **influence** it. This is the most impact you can hope to have on others. We cannot control others, but we can have varying degrees of influence on their decisions.
- You have **no control** over it. There are many situations in which we have absolutely no control.

It is a valuable skill to be able to discern which scenario is at play at any given time. If you assess the situation and recognize that you have absolutely no control, then you will not waste time and effort trying to exercise control. If you realize that you can control a personal outcome, then do everything you can to control the situation to make progress toward your goals. If you realize that you can influence someone else's decision in a way that promotes the greater good, then do so in a positive, respectful manner. In any situation, remind yourself, "I am in control." Say it over and over again…as many times as it takes for you to believe it.

> *I think that if you live long enough, you*
> *realize that so much of what happens*
>
> *in life is out of your control, but how you*
> *respond to it is in your control.*
> *That's what I try to remember.*

—Hillary Clinton

Areas of Personal Growth That I Can Work On

List three areas in your life that you do *control:*

1. _____

2. _____

3. _____

List three areas in your life that you *influence:*

1. _____

2. _____

3. _____

List three areas where *you can* take *control:*

1. _____

2. _____

3. _____

Try not...do or do not. There is no try.

—Yoda (Star Wars, Episode 5)

Nine

Set Audacious Goals

Nothing is impossible, the word itself says: I'm Possible
—Audrey Hepburn

Three Simple Steps for Goal Setting:

1. **Evaluate** – *Start by understanding*
2. **Formulate** – *Possible solutions*
3. **Act** – *Take action*

The Problem-Solving Process

The first step in our problem-solving process is to *Evaluate.* We attempt to understand the problem, where it came from, and how it got here. We identify the components of the problem and find the moving parts. We understand the participants' roles and where they fit in the problem. How does the problem affect us, and others?

Step two in our problem-solving process is to *Formulate.* By understanding the problem, we can find several possible solutions. Some may be easy solutions, and some may be harder to do. Some may require coordination of other people or factors.

This naturally leads us to take action. To *Act* is the third step in the problem-solving process. Of our many possible solutions, some are probably more feasible than others. Is there anything that you can do that will realistically impact a positive change, and that will move the problem toward a solution? Any solutions that you are personally able to execute on should be considered if it makes sense to do so.

Being a problem solver is an important part of the *I can* persona. Find a problem, think of how to fix it, and then do what you can to help the situation.

1. Evaluate

Start by Understanding

Goal is not a dirty word. We want to have some fun with the word *"goal."* What was your first thought when you saw the title of this chapter? Be honest, were you ready to run for the hills? A lot of people are fearful of setting goals. In researching the topic of goal setting, we interviewed several people and many equated goal setting with something painful.

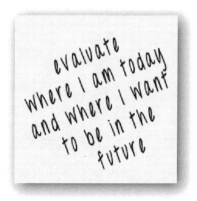

And we don't blame them. In our past readings and research, we found that most of the goal-setting books were overly complicated and lengthy. By the time you got through all the necessary readings and lists and charts, and all of the why and what for, you were ready to say forget it. We have been in situations where the mountains of required work to accomplish our intended goal seemed overwhelming. Our intention was there, our motivation was strong, and our objectives were clear. But, by the time we completed all of the necessary requirements we were discouraged.

We knew that we needed to bottom line this process, and that is why we set out to streamline our journey with a *simple 1-2-3* process to follow. In your following of the three-step process and taking the actions from the previous chapters, setting your goal will be a fun and rewarding project for you. You are prepared to journey forward and make some changes in your life. Here is our plan of action.

Have a checklist. Select goals that will give you:

- confidence
- purpose
- a sense of kindness
- an action plan
- a positive attitude
- enthusiasm

> *This year I am choosing to live beyond my wildest dreams.*
> *I wonder where they will take me.*
>
> —Oprah Winfrey

Take It to the TOP!

We set goals so that we can be accomplished and be at the top of our game. We want to achieve and excel. As with any journey, before taking that first step forward, it's important to review the path you have taken thus far. Before you actually write out your goals and commit to them, let's review three critical reflections. It's *as simple as 1-2-3*! We have created an acronym out of the word TOP to help us remember the important steps we need before we set goals and climb to the TOP.

TOP

T = Take action

O = Own the moment

P = Proceed

Plan a Course of Action

When you set a goal, you are making a commitment, a contract with yourself. But you know that just setting a goal doesn't make it happen. When you make a decision to do something, it is yours to own.

You have made a commitment, and it is your responsibility to take whatever action is necessary to achieve the goal. Your decisions are about your choices because your choices will determine your destiny. With that in mind, dare to dream. Aim for the sky and settle for nothing less than the most brilliant star. That's you! If you could do anything, what would you do?

2. Formulate

Find Possible Solutions

If you went to a bookstore or to the Internet and researched goal setting, you probably would be overwhelmed. Over the years, we have both tried a number of different ways to set, develop, and accomplish goals, and we found that many systems were extremely complex and lengthy. In fact, by the time you have finished reading all of the exercises and processes, you are ready to quit before you even get started. This is an *I can* book, and we don't want that to happen here.

We want to make this procedure as painless and simple as we can, so we are keeping with our *simple 1-2-3* approach. You can make your goals simple or complex: it's your choice. If goal setting is new to you, then be precise in choosing your goal. That way your achievement has a better chance of becoming a reality.

We don't want to settle for small, meaningless, easy-to-accomplish goals, but at the same time we want to be realistic. Our goals must be believable to us in our minds and hearts. As an example, it would be pretty tough to start training to become a prima ballerina at the age of eighty. Define your desire precisely so that you can achieve an authentic, realistic, and believable goal.

Prioritize

What would you like to accomplish at this time? What are you really good at? What are your positive features? What do you like to do? Where would you like to be? What positive purpose do you want your goals to achieve?

This is not the place for humility. We need to see ourselves as audacious, fearless, and in the most positive and productive light possible. What is your top priority? You can find out by asking yourself these questions. What is important about your life to you? What are your top three goals? Prioritize and decide which one you will tackle first. Here is a helpful approach for prioritizing: ask yourself which goal you would choose if you could select just one. If you could accomplish two, which one would be next?

> *Let the future tell the truth, and evaluate each one according to his work and accomplishments.*
>
> —Nikola Tesla

Continue until you have listed all of your goals in order of importance. The answers will reveal a lot about where you are already focusing your time and interest.

What is important about my life to me? What are the top three?

1. _____

2. _____

3. _____

What do I like to do? What are the top three?

1. _____

2. _____

3. _____

What are my most positive attributes? What are the top three?

1. _____

2. _____

3. _____

Investigate

How will you proceed? What research will you need to do? Who can you consult with who has had firsthand experience achieving this type of goal? Is information available online? Is there a class you can take? What are the potential obstacles that you can anticipate and address now? Before you proceed, look at your goal carefully and ask yourself, "What will I need to do in preparation before jumping in?"

Here are some questions to get you started:

1. Will you need to conduct any research? If so, what kind and where? Is there information on the Internet? Is there a class you can take?

_____

_____

_____

2. Do you know anyone who has done this before? Who can you consult with who has firsthand experience achieving this kind of goal?

_____

_____

_____

3. What challenges and obstacles could occur? What can you do to try to prevent these?

_____

_____

_____

3. Act

Take Action

Many experts believe it takes twenty-one days to make, change, or break a habit. Give yourself up to three weeks to accomplish your goal. Understand yourself and where your starting point is. Be clear about your destination. Divide your steps into twenty-one days.

Always give yourself permission to recalibrate your target. Build in daily and weekly checkpoints to remind you to ask yourself, "Have I overshot my targeted goal?" Our ability to have tightly calibrated results is limited by scientific reality, so please don't be too hard on yourself if you are not progressing as quickly as you would like to. We are aiming toward a goal, which in many cases is a giant step for those who have never identified and set clearly defined goals.

The key to successful goal setting is to have the strength of commitment to proceed until your goal is achieved. Chart your course. Aim for an achievable goal, a desired goal, as opposed to an unrealistic goal that you see as far too distant to achieve. The small steps all add up. Take one step at a time, one day at a time, one week at a time, and that will get you there. Taking twenty-one days to achieve a goal is realistic and represents a gradual progression in the process of achieving your final result.

Keep your goal in your mind with daily reminders. Practice visualizing your goal. This is a lot like target practice. You take careful aim in the direction of the intended target that you want to hit, aim at a target, and put the bull's-eye in your sight. The target is clear, but it takes patience and practice to hit the target dead center. With practice you know exactly the spot you want to hit. So aim and fire.

It is as simple as visualizing what the attained goal will look like. You'll need to know what the goal looks like, what it feels like, so you will know when you have arrived. Picture the outcome. The more vivid the picture you have, the more real your goal will become. Play it like a movie in your mind. You need to be able to visualize the completed goal. See the goal as if you have already attained all of your stated objectives.

Check Your Progress
Once you put a goal in motion, external factors often come into play. Check your progress. Are you procrastinating on taking any necessary action? Are toxic people impeding your goal? Did you allocate enough time to complete one daily activity that will aid in achieving your final goal?

Have you set aside time to check your progress on a daily basis? What are your feelings? Do you feel really great, and are you eager to proceed with gusto and enthusiasm you have never felt before? We want you to sizzle with zest and zeal, to have such dynamic excitement about yourself that you can hardly contain it.

Keep your goal and your path to achieving it as simple as possible. As you identify your goal and what the outcome will look like, pick a measurable benchmark. You will follow this benchmark during the activities and action steps that will guide you on the path to accomplishing your goals. Understand yourself and what your beginning point is. Follow the instructions with diligence, precision, and courage.

If it takes twenty-one days to make, break, or change a habit, give yourself up to three weeks to accomplish your goal. As you move forward, you will learn a lot about yourself. Once you have accomplished a goal, you will experience such a sense of fulfillment and passion from this achievement that you will soar with enthusiasm, the limits of which you have never known before.

Review and Evaluate

Based on your progress, review, refresh, and recalibrate your goals. Evaluate what external factors are interfering with your progress and how you are going to deal with them. Once you put a goal in motion, external factors often come into play. Decide if these factors are helpful. If they are, continue. If they are not helping, then take control, refocus, and get back on your path to accomplish your goal.

> *Too often we underestimate the power of a touch, a smile, a kind word, a listening ear, an honest compliment, or the smallest act of caring, all of which have the potential to turn a life around.*
>
> —Leo Buscaglia

Accountability Buddy

In our professional lives, we are very used to setting and attaining goals. When we set goals in business, they are often very public. There can also be others involved in accomplishing our not-so-private goals. In the business world, there can be layers of oversight and outside accountability. What we accomplish, or do not accomplish, is often public. Our goals can have a lot of eyes on them. Just knowing that the goals that we set are not private but indeed accessible to the surveillance of others often provides us with extra inspiration. When others are watching, we sometimes try a little harder and possibly execute on activities that we might have been inclined to put off. Overall, we typically attain a higher level of performance when outside pressure exists. We know others are watching and cheering for us to cross the finish line we have set for ourselves.

We will apply this same system to our personal life and to our personal goals. It is helpful to have an accountability buddy, to check in on a regular basis, which helps to keep us on track. Knowing that you will be reporting to someone other than yourself will bring an added level of encouragement to accomplish what you have set up for yourself in your goal plan. Accountability to others helps to keep us moving toward our goal attainment when we might need a little extra incentive not to put off for tomorrow what we could be doing today.

An accountability buddy can take many different forms:

- This buddy could be a friend you ask to assist you with your goal accountability. Plan to meet with your buddy on a regular basis to check your progress. Maybe you work on your goals together and reciprocate by being an accountability buddy for each other.
- It could be a professional you hire who has expertise in the topic of your personal goal. You should set up a schedule where you meet and work on your goal to monitor your progress. Because this person is a professional in his or her field, your time and energies will be better spent than if you did the same work alone without his or her help. This will get you to your goal sooner.

- You could create or join a group of people who are working toward the same type of goals. This group should meet, communicate, and connect on a regular basis to report and provide support.
- A study group setting may work for you. A study group works toward gathering knowledge on a common topic of interest. They share information and typically report how this knowledge applies to them on a personal level and how it is helping them to attain their goals.
- Accountability partners can also be found online. It can be an app for your phone, smart pad, or computer where you can set and track goals. Goals that can be quantified work well here.

Whether it is for personal or professional goals, it often pays to not go it alone. When there are resources available, it is just smart to avail yourself of them. Work with others who can relate to where you are and where you want to go. Let others help you get there. Typically a positive and knowledgeable influence can be a big plus for you.

Accountability buddies can help to accelerate your goal attainment process and get you on to the next goal quicker. "Solo is too slow" in most cases. Complement the resources of people with your personal research. Seek to be knowledgeable. It is knowledge that helps to create the solid foundation that we build our goals on.

Reward Yourself—You Deserve It!

You could have twelve reasons to celebrate over the next year! The attainment of a goal may be enough of a reward for you, so you may be thinking that no other reward is necessary. We would like to encourage you to do something celebratory for yourself regardless. Even if it is something small, make it symbolic

Give myself a special reward for each goal met

for you. Maybe go to a movie, go out for an ice cream cone, or take a scenic walk or drive.

Once you have achieved your goal, it is now time to celebrate. We celebrate success because we want to be sure that the reward is now a part of the goal for that month. In fact, when you are setting a goal for the month, it is highly effective to decide what your reward will be for reaching the goal as well. The preset reward may give you a little extra incentive. Try to complete the reward during the same month you achieved the goal so that it has, for you, a correlation with your goal. Identify what worked well and incorporate your successes into your reward. You have grown, you have adopted your *I can* attitude, and it has worked for you. You achieved your goal! Now take the fourth week to reward yourself because you have indeed earned a reward for a job well done.

Reflect on Your Journey

Just think, if you were to select one new goal a month, you will have accomplished twelve new things in one year. This is spectacular and something to be very proud of! You may be thinking, "Only twelve?" But twelve identified goals a year is a huge accomplishment, even for a seasoned goal setter.

I can set goals to make my dreams come true

Think about this for a moment. This certainly exceeds what most people typically do in a year. If you set one new goal a month, you will have added twelve more accomplishments to your life in one year. This is a future with endless possibilities.

Where will these new goals take you? After three months you will have three goals attained, after six months you will have six new goals accomplished, and after one year you will be at twelve. In year two, you will have accomplished twenty-four goals, and thirty-six at year three.

At year ten, you will have accomplished 120 new goals! Wow! This is truly a positive and life-changing path that you are in control of. Now at any point on your life's journey you can say, *"Yes, I can!"* You are ready to begin!

> *There are no traffic jams along the "extra mile."*
> —Roger Staubach

When setting your goals the following questions are helpful:

What goal would you like to achieve? What are your top three?

1. _____

2. _____

3. _____

How will achieving this goal make you feel? What are your top three feelings?

1. _____

2. _____

3. _____

What are you willing to do to make this goal a reality in your life? What are the top three things?

1. _____

2. _____

3. _____

How will you prepare for this goal? What are the top three things you will do?

1. _____

2. _____

3. _____

What activities are you willing to undertake to accomplish your goal? What are your top three?

1. _____

2. _____

3. _____

Do you believe in this goal and feel that it is possible for you to accomplish it? What are your top three reasons?

1. _____

2. _____

3. _____

What are your thoughts as you set this goal? What are the first three that come to mind?

1. _____

2. _____

3. _____

What does successful attainment of this goal look and feel like? What are the top three successes that come to mind?

1. _____

2. _____

3. _____

How will you reward yourself once you have reached this goal? What are the top three rewards?

1. _____

2. _____

3. _____

The future will be different when you accomplish this goal because…? What are the top three things that will be different?

1. _____

2. _____

3. _____

Ten

Stop!

As we look ahead to the next century, leaders will be those who empower others

—Bill Gates

As with any great undertaking, we will need to develop a solid foundation and a sound strategy. It all begins with our thinking, but, before we move on, let's come to a full *Stop!*.

Visualizing a stop sign can help you with your self-talk when you have far too much "stuff" going on and feel anxious, stressed, or over-whelmed. Close your eyes and visualize the kind of stop sign you see on the roads every day. Our minds are already programmed to stop at a stop sign, so this is an easy tool to use. Remind yourself to *Stop!* and gain control of your thoughts, words, and actions.

Let's say your workload seems impossible in your job and the deadlines keep getting closer and closer, yet the project is moving slower and slower. You're ready to scream. Sound familiar? Or maybe there's an important event that will be here all too soon and you're just not ready for it. Perhaps you're a parent, or a boss, and your kids or employees are tugging at you from all directions. You're at the end of your rope, you've tied the proverbial knot, and still the push and pull continue from all directions. And as hard as you try to be proactive, the reactive portion of life becomes unsettling.

This is when we use the stop sign visual. Think about it. You might be alone or with a crowd of people, and maybe all eyes are on you. If your mind is in a panic and reeling, and you are overwhelmed, you must get out of that mental place and bring yourself back to the calm center of your being. The key is to snap out of negative thoughts and behavior quickly. Go to your positive place. The quickest and most effective tool to use is to visualize that stop sign and just *Stop!*

Stop and Think

You have the power within you to control your life, to stop all the negative self-talk, and to stop unproductive behavior. How do you do that? Visualize your stop sign. We use this technique often. It is doubtful that you will ever look at a stop sign in the same way.

I will stop so I can start

OK, so stuff happens, you're depressed, you're anxious, you're doing a hundred million things at one time, you're going non-stop, and you feel consumed and lost in the moment. Obstacles keep coming your way. You want to scream. So what are you to do? *Stop!* Just say no! By the way, *no* is a complete sentence. So just *Stop!*

Stop Negative Thoughts

Try to clear your mind of negative thoughts. If those negative thoughts remain, ask yourself, "Who's the boss?" Just say it to yourself, or if no one is around, say it out loud and really mean it. Then hear yourself say, "Stop! I am the boss." Feel it and believe it.

You are the only one who can stop all the chatter that's causing negative thoughts to enter into your mind. Remove these negative thoughts from your personal space. Erase these thoughts. Cancel them. Delete them. Repeat this practice, and do whatever it takes to stop negative thinking from taking over. Remember; with repetition comes success. Negative thinking clouds your thoughts and is of no value to you. Negative thinking is not doing you any good, so get rid of it.

> *Once you replace negative thoughts with positive ones,*
> *you'll start having positive results.*
> —Willie Nelson

Stop and Quiet Your Mind

Concentrate on something that is not personal. Listen to relaxing music or something motivational. Read an uplifting, positive book. Let's say your choice is music. Avoid listening to any music that can bring back negative memories. You want to slow down, to quiet your mind. Listen to neutral music, maybe instrumental only. Try listening to nature sounds, light classical music, or relaxing music. Listen until it stops the chatter of your mind. Be calm and peaceful.

Music can also work for positive energy. Find motivational, upbeat music you associate with going forward and having the confidence to proceed—music you might listen to at the gym or while going for a run. Use this music to aid you in feeling good and to replace any negative thoughts. There is not room for both. It's a good idea to have headphones with you for the times when you need to use music to replace negative thoughts.

Be aware of your thoughts when you are thinking about "stuff": things you need to do, things that are not going well, or things that could go wrong, and on and on. *Stop!* thinking about "stuff"; it's just "stuff," and it will obstruct your positive thinking. Instead, concentrate on something peaceful. Encourage your mind to concentrate on the sound and vibration of the music, or the rhythm of an ocean wave. Maybe it's the rustling of the leaves on the trees as a breeze blows through. Change your mental environment. We want you to concentrate with such intensity on something peaceful that any minutia you're thinking will stop and float away as it is replaced by the relaxing thoughts that are now entering your mind. By seeing the *stop* sign and by saying *Stop!* even if you have to say it a hundred times—soon you will be able to concentrate on positive thoughts within a ten-minute time span. Then you will be able to increase it to twenty and then to thirty minutes. You will be back in control, and you can continue to relax, meditate, or get on with the task at hand.

Stop and Breathe

Stop! whatever you're doing, thinking, or feeling. *Stop!* thinking about whatever has you down or has you thinking erroneous thoughts about yourself. Put a *stop* to it right away. Just *Stop!* and take a deep breath. Breathe in through your nose and let your breath out slowly, very slowly, through your mouth. Do this breathing technique three times and just let go. You will feel relaxed, rested, and stronger. As you breathe, think or say, "Let go, let go, let go," or "Relax, relax, relax."

The purpose of this exercise is to still your mind with whatever words will help you to just let go. This breathing technique is important because it helps you to stay in control and on target and to reduce feelings of anxiety. Practice this every day. It will reduce stress and keep you on course and focused on what you need to get done. It is a great stabilizer.

*Something will grow from all you are
going through. And it will be you.*

—Toby Mac

Stop and Acknowledge

If negative thoughts keep entering your mind
and you feel like you just can't *stop* the negative
thinking, it's OK. Just acknowledge it and say,
"OK, you're there, negative thoughts. I hear
you. Thank you for being there, but for right
now I choose to concentrate on the positive
and simply move on." Listen to your thoughts,
be in control, and *Stop!* the negative thinking.
You're going to have a conversation with your

mind, informing your mind that this is what you are choosing to do and
asserting that you are in control. You choose what you want to pay attention
to, so find the *I can* and move forward.

However, if you are having negative thoughts that are actually real issues that
need to be addressed and dealt with or that will still be there later, ask yourself
if they can be dealt with at a more appropriate time. We realize that life is not
always positive, but if timing is the issue, then give yourself permission to
delay the negative thoughts until a more appropriate time is available for you
to deal with the issue, maybe at a specific time that you schedule.

If it is a matter of urgency or safety, of course, the negative thoughts should be
dealt with immediately and by a professional, if necessary. Otherwise you get
to be in charge of when to deal with such thoughts.

*We are built to conquer environment, solve problems,
achieve goals, and we find no real satisfaction or happiness
in life without obstacles to conquer and goals to achieve.*

—Maxwell Maltz

Stop and Conquer Obstacles

The *Stop!* strategy will help you control the negative thoughts that flood your mind automatically. Sometimes we have a learned response to particular stimuli or triggers. But by using *Stop!* to control our thoughts and to be aware of them, we can halt the negativity before it fills our minds and heart with negatives and before it affects our mood, productivity, or self-confidence. Act smart, be smart, and just *Stop!*

One thing we all have in common is the power of choice. We were all created with the ability to choose. How we use this gift will determine our outcome. Obstacles can temporarily detour you, but only you can prevent the negative reaction to it and only you can put yourself back on your positive and productive path.

Recognize that obstacles and opposition will happen as you attempt to improve your life and accomplish new goals. Some obstacles may be predictable for you, and some will not. But you now have the power to keep on keeping on. Don't get discouraged and quit when challenges arise. Deal with them and keep going. You are in control. The ability to make constructive decisions depends on the choices you make. You have the power and the choice, and it is up to you to choose what kind of a life you're going to have.

Stop Being So Hard on Yourself

Think about it: you would probably forgive someone who injured or hurt your feelings. All that person would have to say is, "I'm sorry," and you would forgive him or her and move on. But you know it's not that way for you. If you hurt someone, even if it was not deliberate, you know you're going to beat yourself up verbally over and over again. Why do we all do this to ourselves? We must

I will not give away my personal power

Stop! this negative thinking. Your friends would forgive you, so why not be your own best friend, forgive yourself, and move on? You have three of the best and strongest people in your corner: Me, Myself, and I. Permission is granted to be your own best friend and continue nurturing the special you that you are.

> *Keep away from people who try to belittle your*
> *ambitions. Small people always do that, but the really*
> *great make you feel that you, too, can become great.*
>
> —Mark Twain

Stop Toxic People

Toxic people love to stir up trouble. They have complaints about everything. They are negative and often angry. They love gossip, and they will suck the positivity right out of you. They can crush your dreams, squash great ideas, and are exhausting. You are not responsible for their actions, nor should you be an enabler. Do not give away your personal power to toxic people. When you encounter a toxic person and he or she starts with the blah...blah...blahs, be kind and walk away. Say to yourself or that person, "Don't put that in my space," and move on.

> *Those who matter don't mind, those who mind don't matter.*
>
> —Dr. Seuss

An Old Tale

My grandmother told me a story about a woman in her village who went about minding everyone else's business but her own. She was the village gossip. One day she was gossiping and insulted a neighbor. When her neighbor found out, she was furious and challenged her.

Realizing the error of her ways, the woman went to the preacher and asked for forgiveness. The preacher thought about it for a moment. He told her to find the largest feather pillow she had and to take it to the highest hilltop in the village. He told her to tear open the pillow and shake out all of the feathers, and then to return. She did as she was told.

When the woman returned to the preacher, he told her, "Now I want you to go collect all of the feathers and put them back in the empty bag." The woman went back to the top of the hill, but all of the feathers had blown away.

When she returned with the empty bag, the preacher said, "The same thing is true about words. They are easy to say, but once spoken, you cannot retrieve them. So be careful in choosing the words you say, and be careful of what words you listen to."

Remember that people will forget what you have said. People will forget what you have done, but people will never forget how you made them feel. Follow the Golden Rule: "Do unto others as you would have them do unto you."

> *I've learned that people will forget what you said, people will forget what you did, but people will never forget how you made them feel.*
> —Maya Angelou

Negative Activities That Require a Stop Sign

- *Stop* letting toxic people into your life.
- *Stop* listening to what negative people have been telling you.
- *Stop* negative thoughts, as they dramatically affect how you feel and every decision you make.
- *Stop* allowing negative energy to steal your power.
- *Stop* and take control of how you feel, act, and are.
- *Stop* saying yes to everything. Just say no! *No!* is a complete sentence.
- *Stop!* Do it!

Value Yourself

Are you giving away too much of yourself? Do you feel you are getting nothing in return? Value yourself. This is important. Please do not give yourself away. Never give away your personal power, because when you do, you give away a part of yourself. You are too valuable for that. You are absolutely, positively too valuable to just give it away. Power up for victory, as the cheer goes, and start working on you!

Now, as a favor for us, do something for yourself. Today, go to a copier and make two copies of your hand. Post the copies where you will be sure to see them. Put one on the refrigerator door and the other on the back of the bathroom door. This way you will be sure to see them every day. Now, as your own best friend, pat yourself on the back for a job well done each and every day. This will force you to recognize your accomplishments every day, of which you will find many.

> *Don't let what you cannot do interfere with what you can do.*
>
> —John Wooden

The Stop-Sign Plan

S   ***Smile***
    You cannot smile and be sad at the same time.
    It takes fewer muscles to smile than to frown.

T   ***Tough times***
    When you make a decision to change, be prepared for opposition.
    It will happen because it is a natural phenomenon of change.

O   ***Opportunities***
    Opportunities appear in the form of people, places, and things.
    Watch for "serendipity." It happens when you least expect it.

P   ***Preparation***
    Map out your plan.
    Proceed with the plan. Trust it. Work it.

The Stop-Sign Questions

List three things you want to *stop* doing:

1. _____

2. _____

3. _____

List three things you can smile about:

1. _____

2. _____

3. _____

List three actions that you plan to take when opposition appears:

1. _____

2. _____

3. _____

List three serendipitous surprises that you have noticed:

1. _____

2. _____

3. _____

List three things that you will do to prepare for your plan:

1. _____

2. _____

3. _____

Eleven

Time to Set Your Goals

*What the mind of man can conceive and
believe, the mind of man can achieve.*

—Napoleon Hill

Before applying our three-step process for setting and accomplishing our goals, we would like to share with you some sample goals. These examples represent goals that we have set and accomplished, as well as some of the goals of our friends, family, and business associates. We thought that you might enjoy a quick glance at some examples before you set out on your journey.

Three Goal Categories:

1. **Personal Goals** - *To help yourself*
2. **Community Goals** - *To help family, friends, and others*
3. **Professional Goals** - *To help your business and career*

1. *Personal goals:*

Learn to be your own best friend

- Strive to live each day, one day at a time.
- One of the best goals that you should set would be to become your own best friend.
- Work on how you respond to how do you feel.
- Remember that only you can be in control of your actions.
- Take care of you. You are not being selfish when you focus on yourself. In fact, everyone and everything around you is counting on you to be the best you can be and to function at your highest level.
- Allow yourself to be in a most positive, productive, happy, and peaceful place.
- Your goal may be to practice and live by accepting yourself just the way you are.
- Do something each day just for the pure enjoyment of it, as it adds to your personal balance.
- Work on your self-image. Don't be so hard on yourself.
- When you set a higher standard for yourself, everyone you come in contact with will be motivated by the standard you have set.
- To be your best self may require that you work on being your own best cheerleader.
- Do one thing each week that gives you pleasure/enjoyment. Do it just for you.
- Soak in a tub, get a manicure, get a massage, get your makeup done, or get a new hairstyle. Read a book just for enjoyment.
- Get organized with your surroundings. At the office, your desk is a good place to start. In your home, work on getting one room a week organized. Start with one closet at a time.
- Work on what you need to do, what you want to do, and what your example will do for others.

- Remember that for good health:
Take Action: Diet + Exercise = Results.
- Fit in that workout. Wake up earlier, walk or go to the gym, and have an accountability buddy.
- Remember to stop and refresh to reset, which equals less stress.
- Take a class just for fun, or sign up for private lessons.

2a. Community Goals:

Family and Friends

- Give a smile, a hug, an e-mail, or a text.
- Be a better listener. Listen twice as much as you speak.
- Help someone else to accomplish his or her goal to be better organized with his or her surroundings.
- Offer to spend time with a family member. Take a walk, play golf, play tennis, or grab a cup of coffee and just sit and talk.
- Set a date night with a friend or family member, or one-on-one time with children.
- Have dinner with family or friends once a week, or watch a TV show together. *Together* is the key.
- Have a once-a-week meeting with friends or family to discuss any and all issues that can be brought to the table without judgment. Make sure everyone has an equal chance to share their input.
- Work together on a home-based project.
- Make a simple chore chart for weekly household jobs, and give assignments to each member of the household.
- Start a book club and meet to discuss the book. Give everyone a chance to select the books and moderate the group.
- Help to care for pets, a car, a yard, or a home for someone who could use the help but won't ask.
- Help shop for someone who has a hard time getting out.

2b. Community Goals:

To Help Others

- Volunteer.
- Do simple acts of kindness.
- Support a shelter for the homeless, abused women/children, or veterans.
- Do something unexpected and kind for a neighbor, or a senior, or a stranger.
- Step outside your box and try something totally new that will benefit someone else.
- Teach a class and share your areas of expertise with others.
- Teach someone how to cook your favorite dish.
- Help out at your local hospital, nursing home, senior center, school, church, animal shelters, or Boys and Girls Club
- Be a mentor.
- Walk a neighbor's dog.
- Read for those who cannot see or are reading impaired.
- Coach a team.

3. Professional Goals:

Business and Career

- Set a good example at the office.
- Dress a step above what the acceptable norm is within your work environment.
- Set a time for accepting incoming calls, for meetings, and for "do not disturb" time.
- Invest the time to improve your skills.
- Practice random acts of kindness at work by doing things not expected of you that go above and beyond your immediate responsibility.

- Do the little things to make someone's job easier, and don't brag about it, just do it.
- Take time to mentor a new or fellow employee.
- If your car is your office, always keep it clean and neat—that's why you have a trunk.
- Be on time.
- Return client calls and e-mails within twenty-four hours.
- Start or join a study group.
- Start or join a book club with colleagues.
- Read or listen to a motivational or inspirational book.
- Increase your net productivity by a specific amount.
- Raise your gross production by a specific amount.
- Hire more staff.
- Expand your business marketplace.
- Start a new business.
- Change your career direction.
- Open a product line.
- Add new vertical markets.
- Increase your number of locations.
- Recruit new associates.
- Learn something new.

What personal goals would you like to achieve? What are your top three?

1. _____

2. _____

3. _____

What community goals would you like to achieve? What are your top three?

1. _____

2. _____

3. _____

What professional goals would you like to achieve? What are your top three?

1. _____

2. _____

3. _____

Twelve

Change

Life is what you make it, always has been, always will be.
—Grandma Moses

Change is the key. In taking this journey you are following a new path to travel on, a path full of dreams, excitement, enthusiasm, and determination to conquer your fears. On your way, you will make some life changes, have some fun, and determine a vision of what lies ahead.

The Power of One...and Then Some

Change always starts with *one*: *one* thought, *one* idea, *one* action. Consider the power that there is in *one*. *One* extra degree of heat makes steam. *One* extra atom of hydrogen makes water. *One* thought made aviation possible. *One* vision created the idea of the Internet. *One* person with a special perspective can make a difference in the world. Some examples are Henry Ford, Helen Keller, Bill Gates, Oprah Winfrey, Albert Einstein, and Steve Jobs. They were all just *one* person who made a tremendous difference. The list of people who have made a positive impact in our world is long and inspiring.

What do all of these special individuals have in common? They all started out just like you and me. They were born, they were little children, and then they became adults. Some had extreme hardship, some came from average circumstances, and some had prosperous beginnings.

The point is, they were just people, just one person. These leaders did not say, "*I can't*. I am only one person," but instead they took the first step, then the next step, and then another, and in each case, others noticed. They found inspiration and motivation to follow and join in their cause to work toward the quest, to achieve a common goal. They all made the choice to make changes. It all started with just one person taking an action that started small and grew to more. Just *one* became millions.

We say, "Everything starts with *the Power of One and Then Some*." Soon, like minds come together sharing the same goal, which equals the power of working together: a creative community, a creative world, working together, creating exponential growth, which all began with one thought, with one person.

> *Never doubt that a small group of thoughtful,*
> *committed citizens can change the world;*
> *indeed it's the only thing that ever has.*
>
> —Margaret Mead

Are you a leader? Do you have followers? What kind of leader are you, and how did it come about? Sometimes fate chooses us to lead and sometimes we choose to take the lead. In either case, choosing to take action is what makes a leader. In all cases, strong leaders see things that need change: a new movement of ideas; a correction to be made; a kindness to be shown; a cause to help others in need, to educate, to learn; or an idea to make something new or to improve and make something better. Good leaders are values-based in all that they do so that decision making is easy and choices are clear. A trustworthy leader easily earns and retains followers, which is important to help make change happen.

Your choice to take on the job of living life and to travel the unknown path, one step at a time, will lead you to make changes. Those changes will lead you on a journey that will change your life and possibly the lives of others. Look at the result that one change can make. Think of all the exciting experiences you have to look forward to just by taking one step at a time, just by changing and accepting the challenge of creating new habits. The establishment of new actions and activities are steps that will lead to results and attainment of the goals you have set. A leader lives by the mantra, "If it is meant to be, it's up to me." Remember, it just takes one step at a time. Your job is to keep moving forward, because change is a good, good thing.

Your Moment, Your Life

Picture yourself sitting at the ocean, on the beach, and watching the waves. The waves keep coming in, each wave new and totally different. And so this continues, over and over: the waves come in and the waves go out. This continues no matter what. As time goes on, some of the waves are getting bigger and fiercer, others smaller and more timid, and others are getting big again. And as time goes by, this repeats, over and over. Now, think of a time when you were at the ocean and the water was still, so still it looked like an ice skating pond: smooth, quiet, and hardly moving. A rare sight indeed. And so it is with life.

Yes, the ocean is very much how life is: every moment it changes and everything is different. Every breath that we take, every action we take, is different, just as every wave is different. Life is ever-changing, because if it doesn't change, then we are left to picture a less desirable alternative.

What if, instead of sitting by the side of the ocean, we are seated by a little pond? There is no movement, no fresh water entering it. There is no activity.

It is trapped. And so this little pond of water just sits there, day after day after day. Without change, our pond ceases to develop; it deteriorates and becomes foul.

It is the same for us. If we do nothing, stand still, with no movement, we become sluggish and trapped, and we will deteriorate. If your life is just sitting there and you're doing nothing to change it, your life will be like the pond. It's going to look awful, it's going to feel awful, and you are not going to be happy. No action, not changing...this is what makes life stagnant. Life is meant to create and grow; your life needs to be in motion. It must change to become more, or it will stagnate.

Everyone handles change differently. But change is truly the natural order of all things. We are creatures of habit, and when we set goals, we are moving forward and changing old to new.

Goals are yours and yours alone. No goal is too small or unimportant if it contributes to your well-being. We all learn by trial and error; some goals we will hit right on target, and some we will miss. But we are creative beings, and setting goals leads to exciting opportunities.

But it is your responsibility to yourself to stimulate your imagination with the necessary motivation that will propel you into action. This is why you set goals. The future is guaranteed to be uncertain, and you don't know what challenges may come your way. The only thing you have to know is that you can handle the changes that occur in the present moment of your life, and this moment is the foundation for your future. Remember, when you 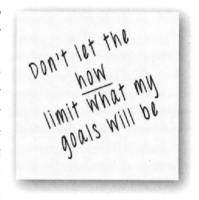 started this journey you set out to build a road to your future, to map out your individual path and start down your own road.

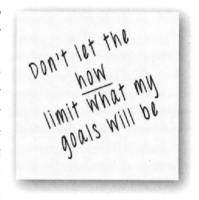
Don't let the how limit what my goals will be

Life is about change. Life is for learning, and we should strive to live an informed life. We live life as smart as we possibly can. Life's purpose is to create; creativity needs change, and with change we grow. Don't let your life be a stagnant pond. Instead, let your moment be that of the ocean. Harness the power of the waves of change. Live your life happy and to the fullest. Give life your very best, and life will return to you the very best that you strive for. So for yourself, for your cause, and for others, say, "*Yes, I can!*"

Thirteen

Carolyn's Story

I believe that we were created to have a personal relationship with our Higher Source as we perceive it to be—a special relationship that's unique to each and every one of us. However, I did not always have that belief system. I did not believe that until I was at one of the lowest points in my life and my current belief system had been shattered. All that I had known to be true, for most of my life, was no longer believable to me.

I was shaken to my core. This was one of the lowest times in my life, and I needed to muster all of the faith and courage possible. But try as I did, the faith and trust that I had in my religion, what I believed for so long, was not working. I could not find the courage or faith within myself. I confided in and sought council from every source I could think of. Every day I would search for answers, for that childlike feeling that I wanted my faith to give me. I wanted to surrender my woes and believe that my path would be made clear to me and that I was not alone in my struggles.

But each day I grew further and further from any faith that I had. I was alone. As the days passed, I felt such deep despair, the likes of which I had not felt before. Then I remembered something I had heard about: *therapeutic free writing.* Just take a pen in your hand and write whatever comes to your mind. You are not supposed to think; just write and let your feelings pour onto the pages.

I had the idea that I would write a letter to God. But I needed a more direct approach. So with pen in hand, I started to write and write and write. Here is what I wrote:

Hi God,

It's me, Carolyn, and I don't know what to do or where to turn. I'm trying to be as positive as I can, but nothing is working. I'm feeling just awful. I feel like such a failure. How am I going to manage? How will I be able to take care of my daughters? Why did this have to happen? Never in a million years would I ever expect that I would be in such dire straits. God, I need some help. I have been praying and praying, but nothing seems to take this sadness away. I'm trying this "writing thing" because I don't know what else to do. So if it's OK with you, I am going to call you "Charlie." I know everybody calls you God, and maybe this is not very pious of me, but I need to get through to you really fast, and with so many people praying to you, I thought it would be OK if I had a direct line to you. I wanted you to know that it was me down here. You see, right now I need help, and I need it fast. I don't know where to turn or how to get help. I need a direct line to you so you'll know it's me. I need to be able to have a one-on-one talk with you. So if it's OK with you, from now on I'm going to call you Charlie.

I don't remember all that I wrote, but I continued to write and write and write well into the night. When I awoke the next morning, I was still in the clothes from the night before, having fallen asleep while writing. When I got up from my chair, the pad of paper that I wrote in fell to the floor. I picked it up and saw the very last sentence…which I know I did *not* write. It said, "Be quiet and be still, know that I am here." That was a miracle to me. As the tears rolled down my cheeks, the anxiety and fear left me, and from that day on I have held on to this strong feeling of calm and peace. I just knew, without any doubt, that everything would work out. This calm gave me the mind-set and confidence that confirmed to me without a shadow of doubt that all would be well. I just knew it.

The "trauma and drama" were gone from one of the most challenging times I have ever had to face in my life. This was an *I can* moment. This calm gave me the peace and security to know that I wasn't alone. I had hope. This alone gave me the confidence that I could and would move forward.

And I did just that. No pity party for me. I took action, and I sat down that day and wrote out three things that I could do, right there, right then. Starting with the basics, for my body, I jogged. I ran and ran. I walked and walked. I did this every day and every night, in below-zero temperatures. For my mind, I listened to uplifting tapes and played them over and over and over again. And for my spirit, well, for the first time in my life I had a personal relationship with God as I perceived my God to be. Indeed, I had faith, hope, and charity in my heart and soul.

From that day forward, whenever doubts or challenges arrived in my life I would have many talks with my friend, Charlie: "Hey, Chuck, I really screwed this one up. Can you help me?" And sure enough, help would arrive. This is not to say that everything in my life has been a smooth ride—far from it. I've had some five-minute pity parties, and like all of us, I have had my share of ups and downs, and sideways to boot! But that day, at that moment, I just knew that I had a friend in Charlie and that all would be well.

This was the first of my Charlie's "Great Miracles." I call this experience my "Zero to Six Miracle" because this was back in the late seventies and I went from zero income to a six-figure income within a six-year period of time. They say "faith can move mountains," and for me, it did.

Fourteen

Daralee's Story

It may be a surprise to those who know the confident, well-spoken me that I stuttered as a child and teenager. I did not stutter all of the time, and I didn't let it impede my progress in high school. I was a cheerleader, a member of the homecoming court, and a top student. Still, it frustrated me, and I lived in fear that it would happen at any time when speaking, which it would without warning.

My life revolved around wanting to say certain words. I would open my mouth, but the words would not come out. I would get stuck on certain words and not be able to speak, or to get past those words.

At a young age, I found the *I can* in the *I can't*. I figured out that there were good words for me to use. I found what I could do, found words that worked, and avoided the other words. Once I could get a sentence started, I was usually OK and could speak, but I had to get started and that was the hard part.

In elementary school, I looked for ways to control my speech by controlling when I spoke. Teachers knew that I stuttered and usually would not call on me unless I raised my hand.

In middle school, I remember one special day in my weekly speech therapy class. My speech therapist helped me to accomplish a day without stuttering. I kept a daily journal and got to write in it: "Today I did not stutter!" This was a very happy moment, as I knew that it was possible to speak, even using some of my tougher-to-say words.

After that, I still stuttered and modified my speech to accommodate, but I was encouraged because I knew it was possible. Life, however, does not usually operate with an on-and-off switch. Change takes time.

In high school, I did a fair job of being a discreet stutter. I hid it pretty well, as I had my words that I avoided and I chose to use the words that worked for me instead. When I was a senior, I decided to go to college to become a teacher. Specifically, I wanted to be a speech therapist and to help others as my speech therapists had done for me. The only problem with this career path was that it required speaking in front of people, something that I was clearly uncomfortable with. As I knew that I had to get past this perceived problem, I introduced myself to the high school speech and debate teacher. I told her my plan and asked if I could enroll in her class, sit in the back, and just observe how to give speeches so that I could figure it out. I asked her, as I had asked many teachers before, to please not call on me. She agreed to help me.

Soon after, our school was hosting a speech contest. The teacher enrolled me in the impromptu competition and convinced me that I had no choice but to compete. I had no time to prepare, no time to develop anxiety over it, and no time to change my mind and try to find a safe place to hide. It was a frightening moment. So I used all of the *I cans* I could muster, and to my surprise, I did well enough in the competition to get a ribbon. I realized then that I had survived the experience and that I could speak in front of groups, and even do so spontaneously. As an unexpected achievement and honor, that year I gave the high school graduation speech for my senior class in front of a packed auditorium.

Stuttering is a mind-set issue for me. I had to find the *I can* in the *I can't*. I had to find what worked for me. I needed to know, and believe, that I could do it. In fact, I have proven it to myself time and time again. I have presented to hundreds and hundreds of groups. Every speech goes fine, and I have never stuttered because I remind myself that I live in an *I can* world, not the world of *I can't*.

Postscript on Our Personal Stories

Life is full, and we have many life events that give us a chance to change and grow. Sharing our stories with others is helpful, as it increases the volume of experiences that people can relate to without having to personally go through those things themselves. It is important to find the life lessons that can help us and others to go forward in an informed and inspired way. Growing together moves us further faster than keeping experiences to ourselves. Gleaning the perspectives of others increases our peripheral view on things so close to us that our perception could be narrowed by that fact. It can't get any closer, in fact, than to be your own personal experience. Sometimes it is hard to see the forest for the trees.

In that light, we have shared two personal stories. They are the past, and we learned a lot by living through them, but they do not define us today. They were part of our life's journey.

Importantly, today is our present. Today is the point from which we focus forward. Always remember that the past can be useful to find positive takeaways that will help you to have a better future.

Fifteen

Exercises and Projects

Imagination is more important than knowledge.
—Albert Einstein

T he Greeks defined happiness as "the joy we feel striving for our potential." That implies that the journey we are on when striving to reach a goal is a happy, fulfilling experience. And that's how it should be.

Exercise #1: Visualize Your Completed Goal

Imagination is a great gift. Children know this instinctively. Why did we ever change the imagination we had as children? Thankfully, many adults have kept theirs alive and growing, because without it nothing would ever get accomplished. Imagination calls for visualization, a technique that many successful people use, either consciously or subconsciously. Define a goal, and then see the result in your mind. Visualize your goal and accept it as

visualize
to
realize

already accomplished. How does it look? What are you doing? How do you feel?

Some people have a problem with visualization. If you do, start small and work toward the completed goal. You might want to close your eyes and see a park. See yourself in that park walking. Can you see the park bench? See yourself taking a seat on the bench…and so the story goes. When you visualize, be as vivid as possible. Watch your scenes play out in color, and be bold. We are trying to make an impression in our minds.

Project #1: The Vision Board

A vision board is a powerful technique and a fun project to do. Some call this tool a dream board or an image board. We are going to call it a "vision board" because we think the word "vision" best describes what we are trying to accomplish. This is the map we will use to keep us on course as we attain our stated goals.

However, what we call it is not as important as what we want to achieve by creating a vision board, which is a picture board you create to represent elements of your desired reality. We're going to make a collage using pictures and words cut from magazines, books, greeting cards, photographs—whatever feels right to you. You do not need to have any artistic ability. A simple picture board of your dream is just as effective as a great work of art.

Using pictures and words, we are going to create the vision we have of our completed goals and use it daily as a visual reminder of goals we are going to accomplish. When referring to this project, we are going use the first-person, present-tense "I am," because it is *your* masterpiece and *you* are in the moment of creating the vision of what success will look like for you.

Materials you will need:

- magazines
- photo images
- scissors
- glue
- poster board

Guidelines:

Any writing you do on your vision board should be in the present tense, such as "I am the CEO of my company," or "I am an award-winning martial arts expert." The board should include all the elements of your goal. It is best to keep it simple. You might want to focus on one area of your life at a time, such as family, career, finances, or health. Or you can include your three systems (physical, intellectual, and psychological) into one picture without making it too complicated. We want our minds to focus clearly on key aspects of our success.

You can make your vision board any size that's convenient for you. You might want to create it letter-size to fit in your notebook or large enough to cover an entire wall. You may want to design a vision board on your computer and use it as your screensaver. I like to make my vision board on a poster-board sheet and place it in my office where I can see it every day.

Remember, you are already there. Your dreams, your goals are bold; no time to be humble here. Have pictures and words that relate to your specific goals. You want to create the mind-set of dreams that are as believable as possible. Keep it colorful and upbeat. Don't limit your creativity. Use colorful images for impact, and try to create a realistic effect. Use pictures and words that depict joy, abundance, and gratitude. Be sure you put yourself in the picture.

Use photographs of yourself or pictures from magazines that resemble you. Place the pictures and words on your board in the order of top importance.

Create a vision of yourself leading the life that you have set in your goals. Put yourself in settings that show you enjoying your new you. Use words and pictures that make you feel awesome to really feel your heart's desire…always positive, always in the present.

Now place your board where you will see it often. You could take a picture of your completed board and use it as your screensaver on your computer, tablet, or smartphone. That way, no matter where you are or how busy you are, you will be able to see the image of your goal to remind and inspire you. Dream about it. Envision the path that will guide you to extraordinary achievement of your goals.

> *I know of no single formula for success. But over the years I*
> *have observed that the attributes of leadership are universal*
> *and are often about finding ways of encouraging people*
> *to combine their efforts, their talents, their insights, their*
> *enthusiasm and their inspiration to work together.*
>
> —Queen Elizabeth II

Exercise #2: To Share with Others

Here are some very easy things to consider when setting your goals. You can share these with others daily. They are contagious, and we just can't keep them to ourselves.

Smile

- A smile is a great expression of your feelings.
- A smile is almost always received favorably, and when it is not, it is usually by the people who need it the most.
- You cannot be angry or sad and smile at the same time.
- Smiling causes fewer wrinkles than frowning does.

Enthusiasm

- Be so excited about life that you live with gusto.
- Encourage others.
- Remember, your enjoyment of life will be apparent by your enthusiasm.
- Repeat every day: "I am so excited that *I can* hardly stand it."
- Pass it on!

Kindness

- Pay it forward. Be a volunteer for a cause you believe in.
- Who can we help? Who can we teach? Whose hand can we hold?
- Have consideration for others: be friendly.
- A simple act of kindness sets in motion a series of events that you may never be aware of but that will bring joy and happiness to others.

Gratitude

- Live with an attitude of gratitude.
- Everyone wants to be appreciated.
- Give recognition often.
- Give thanks daily.
- At the end of every day, count your blessings.

Thoughts and Words

- Every day we give away our thoughts and words.
- Be watchful of the words you say; once spoken, you cannot get them back.
- Words become thoughts, Thoughts become actions.
- We become what we think, say, and do.
- Live with thoughts of joy, kindness, and love.
- Observe yourself without placing judgment on yourself.

- It's a state of being.
- It's not always going to be easy.

Project #2: Keep It All Positive

Use Post-its to Remind Yourself of Positive Thoughts
Put those Post-its to work for you. Write out positive uplifting thoughts, words, quotes, and reminders that will help you stay upbeat and on track. Place Post-its on your mirror, the one you see first thing in the morning. Also place them on your computer, your refrigerator, your office, and your desk—and don't forget the phone. Place these little notes anywhere and everywhere you will be sure to see them. Write positive and uplifting thoughts and words that will help you really feel your accomplished goal. These Post-its will be your friend.

Schedule Your Time
Having a daily schedule and establishing a timeline for tasks can ease some of your stress. Block out time for your personal life and professional life. We all have the same twenty-four hours to work with, so write down everything you need to do. Prioritize your time. Determine what's urgent, what is a must, what is optional, and what can take place later.

Write it down, or put in into whatever calendar system works for you, whether it is electronic or on paper. Whatever works best for you, use it. For some, it will be a simple calendar or a notebook. For others, it will be a paperless system: a computer, tablet, smartphone, or any other electronic device you are familiar with. It is most efficient to have everything in one place so that you can check your time and schedule quickly and easily. Color coding tasks is a big help, too.

Unclutter Your Mind and Environment
Clutter is an issue, whether it is physical or mental, at home or at the office. Removing clutter is critical to restoring order to your mind and your surroundings. It may be physical clutter, where you have a lot of stuff all around you

and you cannot see the light of day. If so, you won't be able to achieve a clear focus. So let's unclutter our surroundings. Work on one room at a time or one section of a room at a time. It might be a closet or your desk. Don't let yourself get overwhelmed. Unclutter one thing at a time, one day at a time. Remember, one step at a time!

Your clutter might be mental—you know, the times when you have so many things on your mind that it's hard to decide what to have for lunch, let alone sort through all the things you have to do and to prioritize what is the most important thing to accomplish. Use the stop sign to keep yourself from feeling overwhelmed and then proceed with your top priority. It is critical to get rid of the clutter and restore order to your mind and your surroundings. It's a new you, so start fresh!

It is your responsibility to own your space and keep it positive. Eliminate any pessimistic attitudes that arise. Trust your instincts. If something does not feel right, don't say it and don't do it. When negatives appear, and they will, quickly say to yourself or to the person who is causing a negative thought to enter your mind, "Don't put that in my space." This works extremely well with gossip, pessimistic people, and negative places or circumstances.

Exercise #3: Don't Beat Yourself Up

When You Feel Like You're in Overload
"Oh, no! I'm in the dumps. I fell off my goal path and let the doldrums in, and I'm really feeling the blues. What can I do?" Setting and achieving goals sounds noble and exciting, but it can tax our already overwhelmed schedule. When the whole process seems like it's about to get the better of you, try this to get yourself back on track.

If you have an off day, go for a walk and invite your three best friends: me, myself, and I. If the walk doesn't work, have a quick cry. If crying doesn't help, freshen up with a bubble bath or shower. If that doesn't work, have a quick snack or refreshing drink. Do whatever you can to feel better and get back on track.

The Five-Minute Pity Party
Just have a pity party. Yes, you heard it here first. When the blues get the better of you, take control and decide to have a delicious plate of depression. We mean it. Feel as bad as you want. You can even make a party out of it. It's hard to beat resistance and opposition all the time, but time is the key here. You are allowed to have your pity party, but remember that it is a party and there comes a time when we have to say, "The party's over." Set a five-minute time limit on your pity party so that when the party's over, it's time to get back on your path to *I can.*

Remember, we all feel discouraged at times. Today it is impossible to know it all or to be able to do it all. The key is to know that with an *I can* attitude, you are more likely to succeed. *You can* do it! Keep your chin up. No one expects you to save the world; otherwise, you would have been born wearing a cape and tights. Just do the best you can.

Project #3: Get Yourself Back on Track

One Day, One Goal, One Post-it
What do you do when the day seems overwhelming and not in your control? A quick and easy way to get back in charge is: "One day, one goal, one Post-it." Now you have the solution and you are in control. How did we do that? We remembered *1-2-3*: "One day, one goal, one Post-it."

If your day has you feeling upset, first remember to *Stop! Stop!* and center your thoughts. Once you are in a better place and can focus forward, think of one small thing that you can accomplish before you go to bed. Grab a Post-it and write down this easy goal. Put it someplace where you will be sure to see it, like on your computer monitor or the mirror of your bathroom.

This very low-tech Post-it system works. You set only one, very easy thing as a goal for the day, and you make sure it happens. You prove to yourself that you can do it! This makes the day manageable and puts it back in your control, because you have a plan, and a plan that you are in charge of.

What if, for some reason, the goal does not happen? Well, the world will go on and provide us with a new day tomorrow. The best thing to do in that case is to set a new goal for the new day and then do your best to get it done.

An example of an easy goal that you could choose is exercise. Set a goal to just spend five minutes at the end of the day stretching out. You will feel good and feel accomplished. Watch the clock and make sure you get it done. The next day, set a new goal, write it on a new Post-it, and keep building from there. "One Post-it, one goal, one day."

This is a good way to warm up to bigger goal setting. Start with one simple Post-it and take it one day at a time. That is how we get on the path to control in our world and move forward from where we are today to where we want to be tomorrow. Life only happens one day at a time; we cannot go any faster.

> *Only those who have the patience to do simple things*
> *perfectly will acquire the skill to do difficult things easily.*

> —Johann Schiller

Have a Pat on the Back Ready to Go

You've encouraged others; now it's your turn. Be your own best friend. The next time you are at a copy machine, make copies of your own hand. Place one on the refrigerator door at home and one on your bathroom door. Place any other copies anywhere you will be sure to see them each day. Now anytime you feel good, special, or you are on track with moving forward, turn around and give yourself a pat on the back for a job well done. You certainly deserve it.

Sixteen

How to Use Your I Can Journal

Twenty-One Days to Your Personal Success

It's a funny thing about life; if you refuse
to accept anything but the best,
you very often get it.
—Somerset Maugham

Life Is for Learning and Living

When you decided to read *What You Can Do...When You Can't*, you chose to travel a new path and to consider new options for how to approach living your life. Optimally, your choices will lead you to make changes for personal improvement and to create new daily habits and activities.

The central theme of this book is that in every *I can't* there is an *I can* and that it is important and possible to identify and apply this positive perspective as we live our lives.

You don't have to be great to start, but
you have to start to be great.

—Zig Ziglar

How to Use Your Journal

To maintain peak awareness about your progress, we suggest using the following twenty-one-day journal in which to record your thoughts, challenges, and accomplishments. This is your daily log. Each and every day for the next three weeks, try to enter in your journal a realistic and honest representation of the actions you are taking to accomplish your goals. It can be as short or as lengthy of a description of the activities as you would like.

At the end of each week, write in your journal what you have or have not accomplished. Persist with diligence to get those tasks completed. This will be your benchmark for the days that follow. As you maneuver through your three weeks, be prepared for the exciting influences that will most assuredly come to pass. Remember, it is said that it takes twenty-one days to make, change, or break a habit. Really, in the huge scope of life, twenty-one days is a hiccup.

Week four is your time to refresh, recalibrate, reset, and refocus. If your next twenty-one day goal is an expansion that builds on the results of the prior three weeks, then you will want to adjust based on if you attained your goal, exceeded your goal, or fell short of your target. How your last three weeks turned out will determine your next three.

Monthly, reset and focus on a new goal

If your new goal is a stand-alone goal, then week four gives you time to put your plan in place and hit the ground running.

Review

Review the past chapters, your thoughts, and your vision of the new you—the *"I can!"* you. As you go back over the chapters, take a quick look at the questions you have asked and answered. We hope that you have changed the way you perceive yourself. Do you have a confident *I can* attitude? Is your purpose well defined? Do you have the tenacity to keep moving forward?

We are being a little repetitive here, but this is your time to be bold and daring. Be audacious and adventurous as you answer the questions. You are in for such surprises and excitement. You are going to gain such a passion for life! As we write this, we feel so good that we can hardly stand it. We are excited for you!

How you feel every day is important. Every day you achieve accomplishments, and it is critical that you recognize and capture them. We want to always focus on what we did do versus what we did not do. Otherwise, it is easy to have a day—or many days—go by when all you do is look at what you did not get done, creating a potentially infinite list of disappointments.

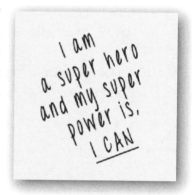

Instead, document what you did get done so that you never fall into that trap. We have found that journaling daily is the best way to capture your accomplishments, your *I can* achievements, and to record your reflections about your progress toward your goals. This is a productive and positive daily exercise. It is your opportunity and reminder to celebrate your wins each and every day. Remember, you can go back anytime in this book and review any section where you may have questions.

Goals Must Be Bite-Size

Remember, only set goals that can be accomplished in twenty-one days. If you feel that your desired goal is larger than this and would require more time to achieve, then recalibrate and break your goal up into smaller pieces. Many small successes will add up to big accomplishments!

Let's Start
Each of the three weeks will flow like this:

- Day 1: Positive thoughts
- Day 2: Simple wisdoms
- Day 3: Intellectual positives
- Day 4: Physical positives
- Day 5: Psychological positives
- Day 6: Lessons learned
- Day 7: Measurable progress

What about week four? Celebrate! You did it! You deserve your reward. Enjoy and take pride in your victory.

After the Celebration

- Create and set your next goal.
- Identify strategies and tactics to attain your next goal.
- Determine your new three-week, step-by-step plan.
- Research your goal.
- Consult with others.
- Create a new *I Can* Twenty-One-Day Journal

Your Personal Success Journal
In this chapter, you will find your *I Can* Journal. This is a template for you to use during your twenty-one days to personal success as you work on one goal

at a time. You can go back anytime in this book and review any section where you may have questions or need support.

This is your journal. These are your goals. This is your life and your future successes to own. Be proud of yourself for focusing forward toward a better future for yourself and others.

As Simple as 1-2-3

Remember our three-step process and keep it as simple as 1-2-3.

1. **Evaluate:** *Set your goals.*
2. **Formulate:** *Aim and proceed.*
3. **Act:** *Monitor and achieve.*

Reward and reset for the next goal. Be proud of yourself and always focus forward to your next success. Just think, if you select one new goal monthly, you will have accomplished twelve new things in one year. This certainly exceeds what most people do. So let's have at it!

> *People say that motivation doesn't last. Well, neither does bathing; that's why we do it daily.*
>
> —Zig Ziglar

"I Can" Journal

Twenty-One Days
to
Your Personal Success

My "I CAN" goal is:

_____

_____

_____

_____

_____

_____

_____

_____

_____

_____

_____

Start date_____

Completion date_____

Day One

Positive Thoughts

I am positive and enthusiastic that *I can* accomplish my goal because:

_____

_____

_____

_____

_____

_____

_____

_____

_____

_____

_____

_____

_____

_____

_____

_____

_____

_____

_____

_____

_____

_____

_____

Day Two

Simple Wisdoms

I can stay on track to achieve my goal because *I can* keep it simple by:

_____
_____
_____
_____
_____
_____
_____
_____
_____
_____
_____
_____
_____
_____
_____
_____
_____
_____
_____
_____
_____
_____
_____
_____
_____
_____
_____
_____

Day Three

Intellectual

I can keep my mental attitude positive today because of these actions:

_____

_____

_____

_____

_____

_____

_____

_____

_____

_____

_____

_____

_____

_____

_____

_____

_____

_____

_____

_____

_____

_____

_____

_____

_____

_____

_____

_____

_____

Day Four

Physical

My goal makes me feel good because *I can* do:

_____

_____

_____

_____

_____

_____

_____

_____

_____

_____

_____

_____

_____

_____

_____

_____

_____

_____

_____

_____

_____

_____

_____

_____

_____

Day Five

Psychological

I believe *I can* accomplish my goal because:

_____

_____

_____

_____

_____

_____

_____

_____

_____

_____

_____

_____

_____

_____

_____

_____

_____

_____

_____

_____

_____

_____

_____

_____

_____

_____

Day Six

Lessons Learned

I can accomplish my goal because I have learned:

_____

_____

_____

_____

_____

_____

_____

_____

_____

_____

_____

_____

_____

_____

_____

_____

_____

_____

_____

_____

_____

_____

_____

_____

_____

_____

_____

Day Seven

First Week Check-in: Measurable Progress

I can measure my progress this week by:

_____

_____

_____

_____

_____

_____

_____

_____

_____

_____

_____

_____

_____

_____

_____

_____

_____

_____

_____

_____

_____

_____

_____

_____

_____

_____

_____

_____

_____

Day Eight
Thought for the Second Week

I am positive and enthusiastic that *I can* accomplish my goal because:

Day Nine

Simple Wisdoms

I can stay on track to achieve my goal because *I can* keep it simple by:

_____

_____

_____

_____

_____

_____

_____

_____

_____

_____

_____

_____

_____

_____

_____

_____

_____

_____

_____

_____

_____

_____

_____

_____

_____

_____

_____

_____

_____

Day Ten

Intellectual

I can keep my attitude positive today because of these actions:

_____

_____

_____

_____

_____

_____

_____

_____

_____

_____

_____

_____

_____

_____

_____

_____

_____

_____

_____

_____

_____

_____

_____

_____

_____

Day Eleven

Physical

My goal makes me feel good because *I can* do:

_____

_____

_____

_____

_____

_____

_____

_____

_____

_____

_____

_____

_____

_____

_____

_____

_____

_____

_____

_____

_____

_____

_____

_____

_____

_____

_____

Day Twelve

Psychological

I believe *I can* accomplish my goal because:

_____

_____

_____

_____

_____

_____

_____

_____

_____

_____

_____

_____

_____

_____

_____

_____

_____

_____

_____

_____

_____

_____

_____

_____

_____

_____

_____

_____

Day Thirteen

Lessons Learned

I can accomplish my goal because I have learned:

_____

_____

_____

_____

_____

_____

_____

_____

_____

_____

_____

_____

_____

_____

_____

_____

_____

_____

_____

_____

_____

_____

_____

_____

_____

_____

_____

_____

Day Fourteen

Second Week Check-in: Measurable Progress

I can measure my progress this week by:

_____

_____

_____

_____

_____

_____

_____

_____

_____

_____

_____

_____

_____

_____

_____

_____

_____

_____

_____

_____

_____

_____

_____

_____

_____

_____

Day Fifteen
Thought for the Third Week

I am positive and enthusiastic that *I can* accomplish my goal because:

_____
_____
_____
_____
_____
_____
_____
_____
_____
_____
_____
_____
_____
_____
_____
_____
_____
_____
_____
_____
_____
_____
_____
_____
_____
_____
_____

Day Sixteen

Simple Wisdoms

I stay on track to achieve my goal because *I can* keep it simple by:

_____

_____

_____

_____

_____

_____

_____

_____

_____

_____

_____

_____

_____

_____

_____

_____

_____

_____

_____

_____

_____

_____

_____

_____

_____

_____

_____

_____

Day Seventeen

Intellectual

I can keep my attitude positive today because of these actions:

_____

_____

_____

_____

_____

_____

_____

_____

_____

_____

_____

_____

_____

_____

_____

_____

_____

_____

_____

_____

_____

_____

_____

_____

_____

_____

_____

_____

Day Eighteen

Physical

My goal makes me feel good because *I can* do:

_____

_____

_____

_____

_____

_____

_____

_____

_____

_____

_____

_____

_____

_____

_____

_____

_____

_____

_____

_____

_____

_____

_____

_____

_____

_____

_____

Day Nineteen

Psychological

I believe *I can* accomplish my goal because:

_____
_____
_____
_____
_____
_____
_____
_____
_____
_____
_____
_____
_____
_____
_____
_____
_____
_____
_____
_____
_____
_____
_____
_____
_____
_____
_____
_____
_____
_____
_____

Day Twenty

Lessons Learned

I *can* accomplish my goal because I have learned:

_____

_____

_____

_____

_____

_____

_____

_____

_____

_____

_____

_____

_____

_____

_____

_____

_____

_____

_____

_____

_____

_____

_____

_____

_____

_____

_____

_____

_____

_____

_____